North of the future

Previously published poems:

'Shaman', *Transformation: Poetry of Spiritual Consciousness*, Rivelin Grapheme Press, 1988

'Tiananmen', *Working Titles*, no.1 Summer 1989

'Conversation in midwinter', *Orbis International Poetry*, no.75 1989

'And joy whose hand', *Foolscap*, no.8, October 1990

'New Age', *Foolscap*, no.10, 1991

'Flatlanders', *Spoils: The Poetry Business Anthology* 1991

'Clematis', *Orbis International Poetry*, no.82, Autumn 1991

'Night travellers', *Westwords*, no.13, 1991

'My father listening to a poetry reading on Radio Three', *Foolscap*, no.13, June 1992

'Bikers', *Various Artists*, no.1, Firewater Press (n.d.)

'Meaning', *Smiths Knoll*, no.10, 1995

'Leaving Olcio', *Poetry Nottingham International*, vol.49, no.4, Winter 1995

'What I Want', *Various Artists*, no.5, October 1995

'Ghost', 'October', and 'Dad', *The Long Pale Corridor: Contemporary Poems of Bereavement*, Bloodaxe Books, 1996

'Poppy', *Various Artists*, no.6, 1997

'The Shower', 'Meaning', and 'October', *FWBO New Poetry: Contemporary Poetry Inspired by Western Buddhism*, Rising Fire, 1997

Stephen Parr

of the North
future

Selected Poems
1968-1998

WINDHORSE

Published by Windhorse Publications
11 Park Road
Birmingham
B13 8AB

© Stephen Parr 1999

The right of Stephen Parr to be identified as the author
of this work has been asserted by him in accordance
with the Copyright, Designs and Patents Act 1988

Printed by Interprint Ltd
Marsa, Malta

Cover illustration   © Photodisc
Design   Dhammarati

British Library Cataloguing in Publication Data
A catalogue record for this book is available from the British Library

ISBN 0 904766 76 4

ABOUT THE AUTHOR

STEPHEN PARR was born in 1946 in Blackburn, Lancashire. At the age of 19 he moved to London to work as a sound engineer with the BBC, and soon afterwards met Sangharakshita, founder of the Friends of the Western Buddhist Order (FWBO). In 1968 he was one of the first to be ordained as a member of the Western Buddhist Order and was given the name Ananda, meaning delight or bliss.

Ananda took a leading role in the early years of the FWBO, teaching meditation, leading retreats, and helping to set up its first publishing venture. He worked as a designer for a large publishing house, before setting up his own graphic design business in Bristol.

Ananda has written both fiction and poetry, and his poems have appeared in leading journals including the *Times Literary Supplement*, and in a major Bloodaxe anthology, *The Long Pale Corridor*. They have also been broadcast on radio.

He was one of the founders of 'The Awfully Nice Poets', a performance group that toured Britain performing poetry and conducting writing workshops in schools, pubs, theatres, and at arts festivals. Since 1996 he has been a co-leader of 'Wolf at the Door', which runs Buddhist-inspired writing workshops around the world.

Ananda now lives in Bristol and is engaged on a new novel in between teaching commitments that will take him throughout Britain, Ireland, and the United States.

PREFACE

GOOD WINE needs no bush, says the proverb, and good poetry needs no preface. Certainly poetry as good as Ananda's needs no preface, and I am writing these few lines only because the publishers have asked me to do so and because Ananda is one of my oldest and dearest friends.

We met for the first time in 1967, shortly after my final return to the West, at a Wesak celebration organized by a Zen group at which I was one of the speakers. During the years that followed we met regularly and discovered that we had many interests (for want of a better word) in common. Besides meditation and Buddhism (in 1968 Ananda became one of the first members of the Western Buddhist Order), those interests included poetry and the life and thought of Samuel Taylor Coleridge – interests we have both maintained down to the present day.

Some of those early meetings of ours remain deeply etched in my memory. There were dark, rainy winter evenings when, after a meditation class, we would walk along the Embankment talking about life, literature, Buddhism, meditation, the WBO, and a dozen other things, and when Ananda would tell me how he was getting on – or not getting on – with the novel he was writing. There was a time when, visiting Ananda at his Kensington flat, I found him sitting in the middle of a floor covered with what seemed like miles of magnetic tape – the tapes of lectures of mine he had recorded. Then there were the days we spent together on retreat on the edge of the Sussex Downs, or staying with friends at a Victorian castle in Gloucestershire. During this period Ananda produced an enormous quantity of poetry. I was amazed at his productivity. He seemed able to jot down a poem whenever he had a few quiet moments, regardless of where he was or what other people were doing.

In the early seventies our paths started to diverge, at least geographically. Ananda moved from London to Croydon and then back to London, while I moved from London to Cornwall and then to Norfolk. More recently, he has moved from London to Bristol (where he now lives), while I have moved from Norfolk to London and from London to Birmingham. We have both travelled abroad quite a lot, especially in more recent years. But we have always kept in touch, and Ananda has continued to produce poetry, though perhaps not so abundantly as before. Every now and then he would send me the latest slim volume, and each time I would rejoice to find him speaking in a more authentic and more truly individual voice.

Now Windhorse is bringing out a substantial selection from his work and I have further cause for rejoicing. Though Ananda's poetry is very different in kind from my own, I have always admired it greatly, and I am delighted to think that the present volume will bring it to the attention of the wider poetry-reading public and win for it many new admirers.

Urgyen Sangharakshita
Madhyamaloka
Birmingham
3 January 1999

CONTENTS

PART TWO   1977–85

PART THREE   1986–98

to all my teachers

part one   early poems

PORTRAIT

Sedately he sits, like an old curate
Sunlight weaving gold into the Chinese silk;
No pretence at eloquence or mystery
Save what is infused by the sun's old gaze.
His friends – those who knew him less distantly
Than most – assumed an air of civility
In his presence, which all too often betrayed
A long wanted intimacy; those less near
Spun tales of dread or might about him to amaze
The dead or drear inhabitants of normality.
Yet few knew the meaning of those signs
Portrayed in secret by his many-fingered eyes
Or dropped quietly in some common worded phrase
And those who did would or could not translate.

So there he sits, wearing normality like a mask
Patting the sad-eyed dog, scanning the headlines,
Smiling at some too-much-handled commonplace;
Who would have thought this age could emulate
(there where Ganges' ancient soul reclines)
A figure long purged of movement, eyes insensate
Sitting with eloquent poise, silent, sedate?

DEATHS

He has lived only
who has died three times:
once in heart (by the agony
of tree and star and fallen
apple blossom), once
in mind (who finds
an endless sea with no land
in every yes and fearful no)
and once in flesh (whose hand
at crack of night entwines
cold and air
where warm and hair should go).
Whose soul these ends survives
grows hot as ice and cold
as fire and new as time and
old as breath
and in these deaths, lives

EASTER RETREAT

Only the wind moves.
The trees surrender whole branches
to the wild invader.
Inside, time creeps with shy mouse steps
sensing eternity unfolding within.

Someone coughs: an avalanche falls
in a remote and unknown valley,
tearing away the clinging veil –
the dim concern of days:
how we came here, where we will go,

our names even are stripped away at last –
the searing wind tears them away
leaving a pattern of countless deaths
a sense of lightness, and the vivid music
beyond the wind's dance

TWO POEMS IN THE CHINESE STYLE

storm clouds roll along the mountain's head
draping veils of mist across dim valleys.
only four days since we parted,
yet the cry of the curlew
hovering high in the mist
brings tears to my eyes
and I find my gaze drifting
unwilled into the west

all day long the lonely wind howls;
looking out from moss-covered walls
I see layer on layer of mist drifting east
and birds hovering high among grey clouds.
how long have I been sitting here?
time flies on the wind, yet nothing moves;
the crying of the trees is like the hermit's laughter:
he has not spoken for ten years

THREE HAIKU

Beside the silver railway
white apple blossom
breath soft with new fallen rain

The old smithy:
wrought iron lanterns shadow
the brown pavestones

The mind at rest; the heart tranquil –
blue and grey cobblestones
in the market square

MIST OVER THE RIVER LUNE

Autumn sunlight touches the ripples with gold fire.
Burnished leaves drop soundless into the drowsy water.
Through the mist the cries of seagulls
their shadows like ghost ships on the shrouded earth

8

FOUR POEMS WRITTEN ON THE EVE OF MASTER SOCHU SUZUKI SAN'S RETURN TO JAPAN, 15 FEBRUARY 1968

1

When you have gone far away
and your happy voice is only a bright memory
I shall gaze through the open window at the moonlight
and see your calm face smiling down at me

2

Winter is ending. Yellow flowers
line the mountain path.
When I remember your happy laughter
joy floods my heart like spring rain

3

The zendo is filled with deep silence
candlelight makes dancing shadows on the wall.
Over your empty seat, wisps of incense float
like ships on the ocean of Buddha mind

4

I asked you 'what is Buddha mind?'
You laughed at my question.
This morning I heard the wind blow in the trees
and saw sunlight dance on the river

BECAUSE

because there is no how or where or when
light flows from the ever flight of sky
because there is no if or was or why
silence calms the never night of then
because the past and future intertwine
all things shine

because there is no this from that to tell
the evening sunlight flits above the dawn
because there's no beginning and no end
the world revolves, still as an unstruck bell
because there is no yours and no mine
all things shine
all things shine

EBONY

Deep, as if it would defy time
yet transient as evening shadows
under an old dry Elm; and proud
as the grim countenance of Celtic kings
whose line is held in awe by stars.
Free, yet haunted by ancient memory
like moss which clings about closed and rusty windows.
Sometimes, a little translucent, as jade
or chalcedony, but never quite long enough
to be defined; once I thought I had it
but some small thing distracted me
and I saw only a light, just about to fade,
and a hint of ebony

THE GREAT MAN

What was he like, this great man?
what power slept in his eyes, and were they
dark or fair?
Was he (forgive me asking)
was he really mad? And did he
really drink wine incessantly?

I do not wish to pry (god
knows) but, what would he say
say, on a fine green Sunday morning
in the quiet park before lunch?
Of course I don't pretend (to do so
would be impertinent)
to have read in entirety his works,
but don't you think – now say
if you disagree –
there's more than a touch
of wit (as was his way)
in the poetry of this great man?

First of all (I'll settle this at least)
his madness
was the madness of a bird
that screeches out its love
upon a lonely rock at sea; apart from this
forgivable idiosyncrasy
he was as sane as you or me.
No doubt he swore, and doubtless too
he drank until his face was blue;
his bills (I hear) were seldom paid, and god

knows where at night he laid
to sleep; and considering (with due respect)
his life, I'd say it was
a bloody miracle he wrote at all –

but then
the reason he was (to put it mildly)
odd, and seemed to us to be (you know)
like Zeus was to old Plato
is certainly
that in this world of pushing
and shoving, and counting the hours
that space us from the grave
he alone didn't – in fact was quite unable to –
stop loving –
and for that love
his life he gave

FOR KRYSTYNA

The sea grows calm with noon's long lingering
And bright-eyed birds deceived by summer heat
Season the air with autumn's song, remembering
May's quick joy which fled still incomplete.
So now their song awakes a second spring
Whose music plays to heart and mind alike
Yet sorrow all the more comes deftly murmuring
That love's young leaves the winter air will strike.

O fragile summer! Linger still awhile!
I fear to death you are that selfsame dream
Which brought her to me, a single month ago,
And I will wake to sad sea-whispered stream
Where seemed to flow the full star-fragrant Nile
With honeyed waters and deep enchantment's glow

THE VISIT

It came uncalled
as a rain shower over
the hill, in blue May;
no shape
of sea-wave or
stream-cooled wood
encumbered it;
no calm voice
or fey memory
of a once-visited glade
mitigated the intolerable thrill
coming uncalled
and unrecallable,
making brimming May
seem wan and childless,
and flooding crass veins
as the young Sun
flooded with grace
the dressed fields
in the shadowless days.

In vain I returned
resolved to conjure again
the obliterated place:
it merely reiterated
the brute fact:
an odour of varnish,
a dark wood-stain
fast dissolving
in the desolate dusk

CRYSTAL NIGHT

The night is rimmed with ice.
The high moon wanes
and darkly sing the stars
in harmonies of shrill violet
softly modulating into silence

At a corner of the field
steel light dimly vibrates
where a white gate hangs mysterious.
A silverness plays over the metal
where the moon has glanced.

On the stones where you stand
the ice has formed again
around your feet, because
you have waited so long
for one who will never come

FOR VANGISA

The moon alighting on the rayed roofs
creates a land of timelessness
conceived in the immaculate moment.

Sunrise, surprising the woods
in a flash of gold
wipes the world free of night
in an instant of forgetfulness.

Your voice, echoing in my mind
like the antique prophet's dance
takes all my thought by storm
and in that conquered land
breeds silence

CAWSAND

A single main road
'unsuitable for motors'.
Veins of steep streets
throbbing with cries of children
climb to the forgotten fields.
A seagull sits by the Smugglers Inn
where the secret evening stirs like a cat,
and everywhere the pregnant sea beats
its rhythms which quietly enchant the town.
The clock tolls on its tower unheard
for time has been conquered here –
overthrown by the slow peal of waves.
As sunlight gilds the red stone
I try to leave, and ascend the steps
but the village clings like coral:
I find myself back on the shore
where shingle sings at my feet,
reproving those which had dared
to question its dream.

Evening now – the moon climbs the air
yet the sun still hangs in thrall
above the mute clock, and the inn
where the seagull sits
forever

ZENGO

'Sit like a mountain.
Hold the universe in your palm.'

He holds the bell as if it were weightless
its eloquent throat speaking silence.

About his robes an ocean laps
craving their caverned peace.

The sun moves warily over his hands
encountering their stillness like an eclipse.

His feet are sistered to the earth's roots
and time steals in awe around his fatherless face.

We sit like islands where the ocean sips
brooding, with the blood of pebbles in our eyes
watching the palmed galaxies rotate.

Above his head the stunned sun halts

AN IMAGE OF TARA BY MOONLIGHT

Her figure glows like pearl, enshrined
In a cradle of mysterious silk.
A turquoise crown proclaims her sovereign,
Whispers her affinity with this regal light
Which bathes her limbs like milk.
Under that potent touch, her heart jumps
And her eyes quiver, feeling the pulse
Near, which first made her spirit wild
And her blood burn with the world's deep grief.
Enfolded now in the quiet antique cloth
She sings until the world's end her lullaby
While the sky floods with rain,
And Spring surrenders her throne with chaste weeping.
And – though I would leave and forget her song –
Her gaze impregnates me like a sword,
My heart suddenly becalmed in those siren waters.

Those who think the goddess died
In Eastern antiquity, or is reduced
To an impotent bronze image safely behind glass:
Be warned! Her power lives too near
For such imagining; or else avoid the night
And the moon's maddening stare,
Lest the blood burns, and the truant heart jumps
Remembering a miraculous birth, long ago,
In a cradle of tears, each one a grief
The world alone could not bear

FALSE MIRROR

KEEP CLEAR OF THE DOORS
KEEP CLEAR OF THE STAIRS

IT IS FORBIDDEN
IT IS FORBIDDEN

TO STAND STILL ON THE STAIRS
TO STAND STILL ON THE STAIRS

TO VAJRASATTVA

In the beginning
before the smouldering sun spoke
fire into the quenching sea
before the earth woke from dreams
of burning
and the stars sang in their temples
with voices of ice;
before the light was divided
and the mind bowed with its yearning
for things seen and unseen
you sat with sun and moon on your brow
knowing neither moon nor sun
and were at peace.

Where seawater runs at dawn
gilded into silence by the sun
you sat, and brought emptiness;
where the ancient pagan temple sits
on the fist of the lone hill
you stood, and brought emptiness;
where the passion of mind and mind
ran like two rivers unchained
you waited, and brought emptiness;
where birth first shrieked awake
in the milk-white cot of the earth
you lay, and brought emptiness.
Emptiness of the eye,
of the unfolding petal of the holy primrose;
emptiness of the ear,
of the muted trumpet's secret shrill;

emptiness of the nose and voice
sending into oblivion the ephemeral rose
and fragrance of the apple in April dusk;

emptiness of the hand's caress
and the surging body's sacred thrill
at the onslaught of known and unknown blood
when time shakes, and the agèd sky stands still;
emptiness of the grasping thought,
the book with its burning eye
which breeds the world and turns again
the dark circle of rebirth and decay.
Emptiness, at last, weary of itself,
falls away, like the shattered muse, and is silent,
unable to speak for words.
The sea glides into the fire unboiled;
rock sails in the caverned sky,
knowing the secret ecstasy of birds;
the primrose sings in the heart of the world
unseen, unknown, unquestioning.

Now the mood is over:
the hungry tide invades again
where the seaweed sips
and the dumb shells cling entranced
by the ocean's hymn;
everything remains unaltered
and forever renewed by the sun's dance;
the tree on the green hill bends,
the wind rips from the sky its rain,
sea and storm resume their feud
and the beginning ends

THE STAR

A star lives in my bedroom
in the secret space beneath the linen cupboard

the previous occupant complained about it
said it gave him dreams

the council workmen tried to exterminate it
with slow poison and regulations
but it bit them, quick as a flash
with celestial and savage teeth

a bishop came and exorcised it
with blank verses from a black book
but it only sang to him
golden, unintelligible songs
with no words

an astronomer came with a flashlight and notebook
to catalogue it
but it burnt the notebook to a cinder
and the flashlight fell hopelessly in love with it

the astronomer was taken away shaking
and muttering impossible
ascensions and declinations

all that was some time ago now
the star is still there
unexorcised
uncatalogued

miraculous
and it sings to me
of unreachable moments of space
unmeasurable music
and unthinkable timeless flowers
but it cannot still the wheel
which burns all around me
in the streets of dust

it cannot still the acrid flames
which live on,
despite the songs
despite the miraculous flowers
and the silverlight calling wordlessly

in the secret space
where a star lives

TO AUTUMN

The season devours the last tapestries of green
revealing mind's immensities
in a forgotten geometry of branch and stone;
past and future fade like sea-mist
while the wan light mourns their decay
in a sigh as old as love.

leaves turn in the crisis of autumn dissolution;
green moves into gold
the fruit of questioning in the darkest night
when all that has been known is lost
in spasm of silent radiance.

branches burn with inner fire
waking undreamt colours from the soil
of our shrouded dreams;
death and birth revolve in the quiet seed
moving at dawn in the mountain's thigh,
and the forest's blood seeps in the earth.

in the falling flood the husks of thought expire;
the fleet of summer leaves drifts on an obsolete tide

MELROSE ABBEY

The choirs of stone are silent now.
Music is no longer required here
where faith has surrendered to restless curiosity
and the wonderless chatter of bored coach parties.
The walls are dying of over-preservation
the lawns cut weekly to the statutory inch;
where altars were, a concrete slab
provides a seat for early picnickers.

Only at nightfall, after the gates have shut
against these transient scavengers of time
does the mist roll down upon the stones
and the trees stretch their hushed branches down
to join the wordless litany of light
which the yawning years can still not desecrate

27

REBIRTH

Just as you're lost amid
the glittering fall
of sound, the heat
shimmer above the lake,
or the flickering
waterfall beyond the beeches

it comes: the knowledge,
clear and terrible
that this is all:
all whispering time is coiled here:
all bliss, pain, revelation,
the bloom and decay of worlds

is branded deep into this sheer
moment, in the invisible span
of a bird's trill
never again to fall so near.
You know it, but cannot
take in the enormous truth,

so you go on
searching through the days:
towns arise, cars, armies,
television; a city looms,
spawning dance halls
and round the clock cafés,

and slowly the mind forgets.

And there is no more night,
or solitude, or shimmer
of sunlit haze, but dust
and the shrill of jets
and an ache of dumb knowledge
where once a lake lay still

part two 1977–85

MIDSUMMER, ABSENCE

Far out, the wreck.
Easy to ignore.
You haven't written:
longing slowly surfaces.

Bills fester in drawers.
Paths are treacherous.
Banks collapse.
You haven't written.

Where to go from here?
Surfaces are lies.
Music seduces.
Talk denies depths.

You haven't written.
I want to forget, but
the fact's there,
I can't ignore it.

Where to go?
The world looks so far out.
I write slowly:
the wreck of longing surfaces

APPLES

for my father

His spade's edge is notched by
forty years of stubborn birch roots.
At night his sleep's laced with dreams
which never get off the ground.

Now he smooths the folds
in the *Westmorland Gazette*
the apples came wrapped in,
tries to piece together news

of football disasters, peace talks
in Lebanon, the Duke riding a coach
and four over the sands at Silverdale.
Nothing fits.

Even his breakfast egg
defeats him. 'Lift the skin off'
she tells him, 'don't dig your fingernails in,
you'll spill it all over the table.'

He folds the paper.
He's gone back
to the virgin days, when ovals of moon
were hidden among rags and oilskins

in the potting shed,
and the high allotments spilled
apple-light like a fanfare over
the moor's folded limestone

ENDING IT

*'The wise must know how awesome it will be
when all the wealth of Earth stands desolate....'
(from the Anglo-Saxon poem 'The Wanderer',
trans.* RICHARD HAMER)

No one knows how to begin. The B52s
have lasers, radar,
heat-sensing warheads,
computer simulation
and pretty maids all in a row –
but still nobody has a clue.

In the desert, a sleep-ridden
North Carolina voice: *Hey you!
Wax his ass, boy! Wax his ass!*

In the House the Minister
knows exactly what to do.
His voice chokes on its own conviction:
our duty's clear: to see it through.

A shallow hole in the sand
continually wells blood,
bright, hot, arterial
as though we've cut something
deep down in two,

crushed something in the earth
on which reason rests.
How can we come back home
pretending we don't know?

To begin, we must end
everything we've started,
grieve for the lost shadows
where we see what's true,

find the silent place
where words can claw back their wealth.

If we don't, we're through

CHEAP DAY

Garden fires flare along the track
spitting through tea-chests and damp egg boxes;
down-at-heel willow-herb waits by tunnels;
tired hollyhocks
look lost at the ends of lanes.

Kids scutter through leaves
or bike through puddles;
old men natter by tumbled walls;
becks brag down hills slurred with trout,
and the shepherd tipples.

Now the rain dithers on roofs and bogs;
cafés bulge with hikers and plump girls
in thigh-high heels and woolly togs;
and damp dogs slink in for sly meals.

Fog rolls; cats drool;
vague crags scheme across the lake;
sheep wail in woods like abandoned dancers
and winter, in a trice, answers

THE SLOW MUSIC

There is a season written for every place and every country;
this is the one always lost between autumn and winter
when leaves are embossed gold on the trees' fingers
and the torn moon slips into the sea's rages.

Who comes here passes out of memory
through homeless lanes and wailing telegraph wires
sees sprouting lichen and hissing gorse
and hags of trees groping stoneward in the dusk.

Yet tenderness also: silky bulls in the hills' cages
licking their fellows into rainy sleep;
ragwort dragging secret fire from sodden foliage
and birds teaching each other by heart
the winter's weaknesses.

I lean on a dripping gate
sensing the slow music of the earth's ages
and the wind lamenting in the wires our lost languages

NIGHT THOUGHTS
FROM THE CRADLE

Michelangelo's 'Creation of the Sun and Moon'

The robe's no good – too much vermilion.
And dear God that left arm!
Muscles like an escaped circus freak.
I'll be a laughing stock.
Where's the old discipline? The icy balance?
Perhaps I've blown it. Burned out.
The Syrian bow finally flexed past its limit.
There goes the bell: another all-nighter.

Alone. Just the fire-boy lolling
amid the shadows of ropes;
The birdsong's stilled, the crowd's seeped home
to the same damp beds and heated arguments.
A dog kicks up a racket somewhere.

The brush dips, blossoms: god's glare
hovers in the plaster
just beyond the stalled fingers.
In the street a pail clatters;
an eager lark curves, rose-tipped,
over the dome's first blush.

It's the day after, and half a millennium away
an electronic shutter aims, gapes,
passes on

LEAVING

for Barbara

It was the night of trout
baked in a flash
of tinfoil;

red peppers, cool plums,
rosé and party games
no one could understand.

Michael reeling in rainbows,
fingers dreaming
a flicker of malt;

Medbh splayed by the fire,
Cherry and harebell crashed out
in a misted tumbler.

You read 'doorways' with unpractised ease,
and I feasted
on your ample rhythms,

vowels supple as wind-washed grass.
Later I dreamed of stones
opening under the river's quilt,

and in the valley's side, almost
invisible, a doorway
I am leaving behind, unopened

TEMPLE CLOUD

What is it that stirs
when we listen
to no purpose

as when the accordion-
player in the square
pauses

and the wash of birdsong
for miles around
quietly focuses?

THE GATES OF PERCEPTION

coming down briefly into this
much disputed kingdom
the first item to note is
the slight haze, like a continuous doubt
as to the size, position or purpose
of anything, as if the universe were
just getting back on its feet
after a long anaesthetic.
Secondly, though the principality
has been in existence (of a kind)
for millennia, our philosophers claim
that nothing has ever happened in it,
nor has any cohesive principle been found
to operate within its borders.
Take this light for instance:
countless ages working up to saying something
then clamming up at the last moment.

Some say this is the whole point:
that it's the silent parts
which are the key: that everything hangs
on what cannot be said. But there it is:
one day onions, the next carrots,
as we say here.

As one of your poets has finely put it:
if the gates of perception were cleansed
everything would appear as it is – purple.
Of course, some of our philosophers
would dispute that

DATA FOR THE TRANSCENDENTAL MATHEMATICIAN

For a start, multiplication's out:
merely extrapolate (mentally) the implications
of integrating our base functions:
periodic sinusoids insidiously perpetuate
oblate, miasmic ciphers.

Then division must be single-mindedly eschewed:
(this subtle calculus abhors
the breaking up of noble integers).

Consider now (from data empirically compiled)
the conditioned mind as a spurious arithmetical
progression, a point wandering randomly
between ineluctable limits
its roots imaginary
its terms irrational
its constants wild

The liberated mind, in stark contrast,
progresses logarithmically heavenwards
in spiralling hyperbolas of light
all vectors passed
all circumspheres transgressed
all postulates annulled
tending asymptotically towards
a transcendental attractor

EARTH STATION

The throb of ivy up an Elm bole
seems an impossible permutation.

'What are you?' the glittery voice asks.
'Are you recorded?
Are you in rings and corals?
Are you a signal?
Are you a clutch dropped from the sun's madness
or a pause between cavatina and scherzo?'

Are you a skip from the moment
the universe first saw itself,
or the shape the wind has been driving at all night
in its ghost-wrestling with horizons?

Then, through the bone, a longing
to edge back to the robed gloom,
to unwind reason to its first wilderness
before protein, silicon, spiral, diastole;

then the evening is kneeling
with its necklaces of rose and indigo,
its windless limestone,
the soft globes leaning

THE YEAR TURNING

in the linked profiles of hawthorn and dog-rose
crouched over rock
with their armfuls of glowing filaments

in slate voices slagging the bus service
at the hill's foot, that have survived
silences nine foot deep at midday.

in rags of convolvulus slack between alders,
ice-glint of paths slinking upwards
to a swaying stare of owls.

in warped farm gates, and whitewash
losing its grip on brickwork indifferent
to the salt storm lashings

in draped lights kindling sill and lintel
masks of faces set wordlessly homeward
and in my deepening need to celebrate these things:

seed-swell, sun swivel and fall,
logic's loss,
swift rivulets of dark at last linking us

RAIN MAN

What's needed is a damned good downpour you say
as you rip open the week's mail.
Ten o'clock: the heat hangs like a claw
over the arid garden. You are restless: this
is not your season. You snatch up the *Observer*
knowing it will only confirm your view
with death tolls, riots, drownings,
conflagrations.

All around us summer has positioned
his decoys: kodachrome farms flicker
on and off in shifting green rectangles.
Laburnum hangs listless over a low wall
and already the nettles are waist-high, motionless
against the corrugated flanks of barns.

But you will have none of it: you smile,
shadows drop like rust from your coat's folds.
It will be a good summer you say,
look at the clouds gathering

47

BONNINGATE

They sense my approach
through the thick smoky glass of the greenhouse;
They have ignored me so far:
they are busy with their rich telemetry
signalling across the rippling wax insulators.
I peer across a singing distance of air
at their piled hives, their high villages,
their rarefied, thriving temples.
He is kneeling at the opaque slits
hermetic in grey lead, nets and asbestos,
the high-energy physicist, alone, listening
as the death-dance of electrons grows.
He is easing aside their grilles
revealing the acrid heart of the ovens.
There are colours there that are death
to the civilized eye: raw golds,
plutonium white, cadmium infernos,
the savage blue of caesium;
colours not meant to be revealed yet,
until we have jumped out of our sleep-sockets
abandoned our bone labyrinths
for the pure spaces, the whispered inheritance.
The shields down, the golden radiation pours out:
he slices it off in slabs a megawatt thick,
the charged bodies still clinging, gorging,
and heaps it into his deep box.
Their frenzied language stabs his ears uselessly.
They are not concerned with knowledge, but with
the bright necessity beyond it:
survival. Persistence. Increase.

He hurries from the humming madness.
Their frequencies are dark to us,
their rhythms appal;
their gold syllables melt our logics
though we sink them deep in the memory's core,
our granite oblivions

NIGHT TRAVELLERS

after reading Heidegger

A glint of chrome, far down
the valley. Then
the mosquito surge of mopeds
staining space as they round
the summit.

Twilight comes, with its
winged radiance.

Everything speaks, he said.

Granite slabs, speckled
with one-way mirrors, as if
inhabited.

Blue butterflies in the hedges
a luminous clerestory
patterning stonework.

Now, an edgeless presence,
the full moon moves over her land
renaming everything,
her light a lace gateway
for the bereaved night travellers.

Phenomenology, he called it:
the speech of light,
the new knowledge.

I stand a long time, feeling the cold tide,
the spectral outrider

CHANGE

Last night a full moon gutted
with shards of fear, drownings,
wrecks of disgraced gods.

Now, through a café window
I watch the noon sun arc
across a parked Sierra's convex
heat-stressed windscreen
as ladders of molecular colour
unfold, dance
and mutate in zones of brilliance
like a sense of something becoming possible
against all odds.

I wonder it has taken so long to walk
to this place, shed
the dead syntax,
wake and feel each frequency
stretch
and sing inside, like hope,
like forgiveness

TEA IN ST COLUMB

He offers a menu,
apologises for the flies,
the slim choice of cakes.
Outside, cream sunlight
articulates the blue
angles of flags against
whitewashed pediments.

Behind me an urbane murmur
of musicians discussing baroque
politics and authentic
interpretations of Handel.
The cellist in cerulean silk
deckled with lace, orders fruit
scones and Earl Grey.

The place seems decked
for a festival:
steps scrubbed, gates
painted, cottage gardens
polished to the roots.
But the weather's breaking:
clefs of cloud congregate;
overweight raindrops applaud
politely in the empty lane.

I move on
as the grey skins are shed
listening for the squall
of new notes,
heavy ghosts tumbling
across the moor, the drone
of wet wind
through a rusted gatepost

IN A BATH TEA-SHOP

with apologies to Sir John Betjeman

'That's poetry is it?' said the old boy
with the *Telegraph* and a glass of milk
at the table by the window. 'Well
you can keep it. My daughter's horse
shits better stuff than that.
I just hope you're not getting paid for it
out of my poll tax.
One thing you people never talk about
is how blokes like me were gassed
in Belgium so Arthur Scargill and his ilk
can roam the country scot-free
mugging the economy. Somebody ought to put
one of them tyres round his neck –
that'd be one less fruitcake
for this country to deal with'

THE FORBIDDEN ANGEL

Angel, my heart is in silent uproar:
Your spilt blood paints the sky with pale roses
Dropping into the evening its dark, poisoned wine.
Yet still the earth is dancing with wild, abandoned happiness.

Reeling in oceans of illicit perfumes we
Might have made love amid titanic memories,
Or danced among fairies with sapphire wings
Where fountains fall, cool and echoing.

Because I did not dare to speak
Your shadow flits like a moth over this derelict garden
Showering it with darkly burning rubies
Which scorch my flesh with soft and speechless flame.

Because I did not dare to fly
The sky mocks me with its purple poison,
Mocks with laughter like silver tinsel
Glittering mercilessly in your dying flight.

Angel, because I denied you entry
Into my dark and secret sanctuary
Like a criminal with torn and bleeding hands
You float now through my forbidden memories
Like white blossom falling out of season,
Bringing me this quiet, unbearable sweetness.

Angel, you are my inmost tenderness;
You have come bearing the last rose of the year
Into this forgotten garden
And I have denied you;

Angel – come down once more, through
The thickening, frost-rimmed mists;
Come down into my slow, unhealing heart;
Come down: touch me

IN THE TATE GALLERY

The walls leer madness at us and we grin
Safe in the knowledge that it is 'only art'.
The darkness of invisible angels creeps
Beneath the black seats of imitation skin
Where mild sightseers busy themselves
With catalogues and alligator handbags:
There is no moon sailing frantic
In the gold and violet sky;
There are no primeval forests reeling
In becalmed suburban gardens;
There are no serpents, no enchanted stags
Calling from azure mountaintops;
No midnight festivals of carnage
Leave their bones on our white doorsteps;
Here, art is properly contained
In ventilated galleries, and neat lists explain
Its longing blood with bibliographies
And comfortable dates. But Oh!
Where are you, centaur and gryphon!
Where are our unicorns, our dragons glittering?
Where our moons mad with imaginings
For which the starved heart waits in vain?

AUTUMN CROCUS

You left, as you had come,
with dim eyes, sorrowing;
as the bright train pulled away
from the broken platform, gilded with leaves
no voice uttered words grey
with conventional parting; the birds wheeling
from sighing pines were dumb.

Returning up the hill
amidst leaves frail and obsolete
I saw the autumn crocus glow
behind the façade of the green hedge
like a fall of untimely snow;
and children running with eager feet
by the garden bright and still.

Wild harmonies of wings
tremble as the moonlight fades
and the stars foregather, listening;
though your music flies to derelict shores, unheard,
echoing our parting
its magic weaves among these hushed glades
and my dumb heart wakes, and sings

SUKHAVATI

Walls, broken windows, plaster,
noise of hammers,
shouts from high above
hidden in roof-beams; a sense
of urgency everywhere.

Waking at sunrise to sounds of traffic
brawling below in already hot streets;
meditation bell, yellow candles
glowing like animal's eyes through
the dawn mist of incense.

Creation, where before was merely activity;
harmony, where before was noise;
silence, where before was an absence;
building, where before lay a waste
of unguided stone.

Sukhavati rises; a building begins to live;
people wake with dawn in their eyes
stretch towards each other,
bewildered by this unplumbed
mystery of new growth.

We reach towards each other through parting
mists of our past, and look upon this sudden
fructification of an ancient vision;
upon these flowers, faces, walls
bright with morning sun

remembering, often unbelieving,
how far we have come:
how many ghosts encountered,
battles endured, deaths
and births undergone;

and seeing, all through this
lotus-white morning
the unfathomable
stillness of an ancient face
gazing forever inward

TO VAJRADAKA

Unbridled spirit!
leaping the corridors of the most secret air;
harlequin of colours,
magician of the obedient shadows, tamer
of all that floats and hovers free;
like a king with many crowns
you walk the abundant earth,
and time throws open his jewelled cavern
for your inspection; still you dare
discuss eternity with road-sweepers, clowns
and tramps, and bare
your soul's rubied labyrinth,
delved by spirits of ancient rock and fire,
to the glance of dull incomprehension.
O scaler of the sky's blue turrets!
grasper of enchanted spires, grazed
by undawned suns! the bewildered world awaits
the clatter of your chariot
down shadowed streets
where no star's fires have blazed;
and sleepless, rainbow-eyed
children press the window pane,
feeling the magician near
who speaks with demons, summons
angels with visions in their hair,
conjuring the void

WYCHWOOD

Out of this burning wood at nightfall
come the wounded, one by one
stealing like wind through withered hedges.
As the sun sinks crimson
dying into the purple wreaths of trees
come the forgotten, in their hair
dim garlands of dying roses,
their faces broken by searing winds
lost eyes remembering;

                     from the throng
comes an old woman, bent
like night above the gaunt treetops
who turns and speaks:

                 'though the road burns,
though morning beckons with white fingers,
out of this lost beauty I must scream joy;
out of this wound I must carve roses'

As I turn to go, the night
brushes across the amazed face
and murmurs: 'she is your future'

OCTOBER

Again, it is beginning:
the year's destined holocaust,
spring's film noiselessly unwinding
sliding backwards over the golden spools
as we live again our ancient earthlessness.

At first imperceptible
slowly the wide mornings fill with mist
the dawn air hung with curling, violet smoke;
dusk hovers more longingly,
moves more keenly over our secret sense.

Then the full-fleshed leaves reluctantly undress
delaying till the last impossible moment
the dropping of the gilded tapestry;
the rim of gold no wider than a breath
conjures from the earth this other rainbow,
deeper echo of spring's unlettered light.

Slowly the thin flesh yields,
the golden scythe invades the lanes;
the stretching stage is emptied of its hues
the patched cloaks heaped up out of sight;
all the strange, useless furniture of June forgotten
in this magician's tale of slow enfolding mist.

What are we to do with this untouchable autumn,
this encroaching sea of whitening obscurity?
How live with this ragged scratching beast
waiting in the wings of blind May festivals
or lolling at the roots of leaning hollyhocks?

The graveyard lanterns hissing in the dusk
unflesh the soil of its frail deception;
the crumbled stone where centuries have lapped
breaks in a thousand leaping tongues
and lichen gleams gold on the fissured gate

While the unbeaten heart listens secretly, as blood
touched by the sun's dust-winged revelation
glides in its box like a laughing fish
and through its speaking clock
wild music roars
chiming out of mind its high languages
bright as banished Christmas dragons
and within our flesh lost centuries awake
as inch by inch through the starred dust
the forbidden sun unspeakably soars

FOR GUNAPRABHA

You left, at last, suddenly
pulled by those dark, searing voices.

You pulled on your jacket, stuffed
with blunt pencils and Shakespeare's sonnets
and ran, pursued by clouds of crows,
and voluptuous April woods
singing into your naked brain their
intolerable music.

You left like a prince awaking
from the night's deep, to see
bridges burned on every hand,
and stars staring like insane kings.

You left.
Now, over blue woods
the crows circle, their shadows making
black cavern mouths in the earth
and vainly the haunted spires siren
across an indifferent ocean

BLANK VERSES

for Padmaraja

Poems scratched breathlessly in blinding pages
snatched photographs of a child's reflection
music captured faintly in underground pails
by sharp morninglight are revealed to be empty
of all reason:

the milky pages naked of words
the unfurling oily film empty of images
the buried pails harbouring nothing but spiders.

We awake from night's steep languages
into a further dream of unreachable emblems
silently turning them for hidden signs –
brief hieroglyphs glint in lampblack
faces traced by faint star fingers fade –

longing to stumble upon the secret latch
where the dumb universe springs apart
and tumble headlong down familiar steps
into golden poppyfields of soft childlight

THE PAIN

Imagining it is only the heartless scream of lorries
knifing by me like demented crows
I turn aside, seeking the stillness of some unfrequented lane:
but the pain remains,
the pain remains and grows

Imagining it is only the fading of high summer
through the emptying windows of the hedgerows
I think of spring's resurgence in immortal song
still the pain remains,
the pain remains and grows

Imagining it is only the bite of the October wind
I turn up my collar, and ride till evening glows
seeking the solace of trees still dressed in green
yet the pain remains,
the pain remains and grows

Imagining it is only the loneliness of exile
in a country which has forgotten its ancient heroes
I study history and philosophy – but in vain:
the pain remains,
the pain remains and grows

Forgetting that the heart's loss may be assuaged
only when some bright, unearthly passion flows
I lose myself in the falling of auburn hair across apple-white
    shoulders
so the pain remains,
the pain remains and grows

Forgetting that long-vanished friendship is regained
only upon the high paths where selfless action goes
I search like a beggar through cloaked and daggered woods
or gaze where the swaying pine tree blows:
and, despite my tears, the pain remains
the pain remains and grows

AT LOCHWINNOCH

O time!
Though you count out to me
all through the night
your endless hoard of hours
it is but vanity
compared to the infinite
moment of these thoughtless stars

THE RIVER MAIDEN

I had a dream:
you lay beside me
in midsummer moonlight:
your body as I watched became empty
your skin a shape of pure river water
glinting as your breathing rippled it.
You looked towards me, murmuring;
a tress of bright green moss fell
silently; I felt a smile – no more
than a change in the glimmering –
then saw with grief the vision
vanishing, leaving
unquenchable emptiness.

Now, in the quick daylight
nothing remains but a stream
murmuring
the light lingering
the vanishing, vanishing

THE SPIDER IN THE HEART

The spider in the heart can not be killed.
No earthly blade that seething shape will slight;
Only his rage may be touched at last, and stilled

The venom that from stricken mind has spilled
May nourish imagination's roots in spite:
The spider in the heart can not be killed.

The madman in his aching shade unwilled
Cannot be cut from that deep web by might:
Only his rage may be touched at last, and stilled

The lover, frantic to have his starless heaven filled
Turns in dark terror from the blinding light;
The spider in the heart can not be killed

The infant, in the weaponed world once drilled
Trembles within the haunted lanes of night;
Only his rage may be touched at last, and stilled

The singing peasant in the sunlit field
Knows the agony of drought, and dearth, and blight;
The spider in the heart can not be killed

Useless to brand the ass to make him yield:
His riven mind will dive deeper out of sight;
Only his rage may be touched at last, and stilled

Words empty of breath may be blindly shrilled
To bolster up a dream, or doctrine trite;
The spider in the heart can not be killed

The soldier, dazzled by sun on golden shield
Sees his dream dissolve in painted starlight
Only his rage may be touched at last, and stilled

Our mortal sense is in eternity unskilled
And lures the infirm heart to forms less bright;
The spider in the heart can not be killed:
Only his rage may be touched at last, and stilled

ELY CATHEDRAL

Did those moon-eyed masons ever conceive
in the yellow dawning of their vision
their cradle of new-born brightness
could be a tomb, where imagination
like a wraith goes darkly grieving?
Where song like a beggar wanders eyeless,
and angels locked in stone behold
the lark of faith made skyless by a dream?

ALDEBURGH BEACH

in memory of Benjamin Britten

The waves dance, crested with quiet lightnings;
over the white horizon a boat hovers,
a rising spiral of smoke above the skyline.
The noon sun glares from blue paintwork
flashes from stones where empty nets are spread
harbouring their haul of wet and writhing shadows.
The morning drifts idly into the past
as the pounding tide recedes over black seaweed

and coiled blue ropes; and beneath it all
the vanished voices moan, remembering
what cannot be remembered: the bereft boy
wandering forever through furious waves
and the banished boatmen, rowing out to sea
pursued by the hounding, ravenous foam

REPORT FROM CARNMENELLIS

Walking down this track, I suddenly realize
I do not know this place: stones, sky, vegetation,
trees: all feel alien and somehow false
as if they'd been slyly substituted for the real thing
one evening, when the Sun's back was turned.
The buildings especially: they lean crazily
slopping their roofs into hedges and dank ponds
while a barn by the roadside burns with brilliant vegetation:
orange lichen, green moss, purple foxgloves
glow like deep-sea creatures in this yellow light
gradually evicting the unnecessary fabric
until it gives in, and becomes a barn-shaped multicoloured
plant, heaving its rich sap through the forgotten lanes.

The wind hungering over the wasted walls
bellows the few half-syllables it has learned
during its nine-hundred million years on Earth
and zithers headlong through the flayed grass
snorting, but never finding its prey.
Everywhere the shocking images, the raw nerve,
the winking eyes, the thinly disguised skulls,
the scarlet fungus which sprouts towards me
unzipping its soft thighs, as I try to be
a casual observer at this thundering, prehistoric circus.

I have come blundering to the centre of the world's whirlpool
bringing suitcases full of cheap clocks and encyclopaedias
for which not only is there no market, but no concept;
I have crept into the domain of the blind wind,
into the feral, neolithic enclosure,

bearing trinkets which are a laughing-stock: see
the tin-mines on the horizons staggering with glee!
hear the shouldering rivers tittering in their shallows!

Yet – I am not entirely a stranger here:
there is something distantly familiar in this shuddering
wilderness where the insane churches keel;
there are webs stretched between these wet walls
and the rich stars; webs with faint voices
which the reservoir like a flat, blue ghost, echoes
in the lap of its sleep, as my livid, tangled wounds
imperceptibly heal.

'We must record love's mystery without claptrap'
says Patrick Kavanagh; I wish to record the school wall
in Darwen, with its particular kind of moss
which dripped cold jewels after rain; the tadpole well
fathoms deep in slime and gaping mystery; the cobbles
and the hot tar in summer, which made momentous
irremovable symbols on the smooth stone;
the cracked willow and the stacked apple-box towers
stretching infallible into the transparent night.

Old seventy-eights my father kept, their strange
meaningless titles wailing on the label like a charm:
Uncle Tom Cobleigh, Nymphs and Shepherds,
Polly Wolly Doodle; Gracie Fields, George Formby,
Stanley Holloway, all pressed into my memory
down to the last, cracked, shattered detail.
Uncle William with his false pockets full of white dice
and multitudes of black pens; his bright, ticking
watch, which he sprang to my attention

clicking its wheels and polished as a soldier;
his half-crowns like carved moonlight
which he slipped to me, heavy as mercury
when the dull world wasn't looking;
his sad forgotten conversation groaning
over the dinner table on his solitary visits,
obsolete and pale as moths.

All this
among the sloping streets of mills
the berserk belts of the looms
the hard, heatless light over the slate quarries
and at night, the stuttering clamorous flight of wagons
in the distant shunting yard, out towards Blackburn.

So nine years after, to London;
to pale pastel sunsets and the shadowless sodium glare;
to bedsitters in Baker Street and Maida Vale
where on Sundays the canal barges lingered.
A room in Wandsworth where the landlord played
late Beethoven quartets and cultivated peonies;
Stockwell, Norbury, Streatham and South Kensington,
loneliness, boredom, the odd passionate affair
with library assistant or landlady's daughter;
Mozart, Shostakovich, Dostoyevsky and Van Gogh,
Dylan Thomas and T.S. Eliot recited in the bare bathroom
at midnight: 'This music crept by me upon the waters'
and on the Bakerloo line and in the bus queue,
in the damp launderette on Saturdays, and at four a.m.
on night-shift in the BBC canteen, where the walls
of sagging plaster hold
inexplicable dullness of Etonian beige and green.

Now, at thirty-six, to this tumbled Cornish wilderness
to the wild alien light on the TV tower –
(which at night looks like a Martian invader
eerily piercing the mist with death-ray eyes)
and the telegraph wires harping their unguessable messages
over the miles of sodden, indifferent moor.
After six days of storm,
six days of the wind cursing and mouthing
black fury in its hutch of grass and granite
everything basks in the warm lemon light
which the languid Sun drapes over the hillsides
like delicate scarves of yellow silk;
rocks lie flat on their backs in the fields
sleeping off their nights of roaring;
each small sound pulls behind it acres of clean silence;
bedraggled sunflowers lean toothlessly over hedges
and occasionally a ghostly hollyhock towers
standing sentinel by some weed-deep garden gate
its lanterns gone, its long hands withered into dust.

I know this place now: you can no longer fool me
with your potted peonies, your well-scrubbed hotel steps
and your smiling pixie door-knockers.
You are Osiris, the shattered god whose limbs
still glint in the gnomed gardens of tawdry boarding houses
when the season's over;
You are Dithyrambos, the Goat, balanced
on the high crag, after the last city has fallen;
You are Selene, fragrant and mirthless,
rising triumphant out of the grey sea-mist;
You are Night, the Imageless,
breaker of time's long-disciplined legions;

You are Wisdom, circling beyond conception
in your whole rainbow
your turquoise and opal necklace
your thin veil of shifting silk and sidereal music.

I know you and your ageless disguises;
I know you and bow down to you
knowing the wild darkness you have come through
to reach us, on your infinite journey

FIRE SERMON AT
THE AUTUMN EQUINOX

White straw month.
Overnight, the rich seeds are gone.
Fields smoulder in acrid islands.
Soil heaves dark flanks, and settles.

Smokes stumble among the stacks
Blind, without shape;
Titans that have forgotten everything.
Stones in the hollows keep their cold, adamant.
The sun slips; a wan orange wedge
Clings to the wall; the wood spins oxygen.

Now the burnt fields are filing in;
They wait at the window ledge like war cripples
Their stumps gape sickeningly.
But I have no answer to give them.
The Earth is coming apart, the scenery incandescent
I feel the house go up, a dumb, oak inferno.
I shudder. Heat rings me.
It is the end. The tongues sing,
Their hunger unappeasable.

Something has passed over.
In the smoky light
A door I had not noticed before
Hangs open

FIRST DAY IN THE WASP KINGDOM

I have arrived, and still no instructions.
Only the torn poppies by the roadside
Holding up their red lamps

A garden of tame jokes: winking rabbits
Smoke falling sideways
The willow's laughter fading;
all day long the swallows loop the sky, looking for
   a flaw:
there is none.

The wood hums like a power house
I look for the hidden generator
It is the amber priests circling
Revolving their gold codes.
I listen: a thin fear ripples
But they ignore me: I am the wrong pattern
I'm not in their book of rules

Towards evening, the report of a gun in the woods.
The magician in his leaf-mask stirs,
Cracks open the full moonlight:
It trickles down the sky like sheet lightning
Back-lighting the firs.

The owl does not applaud:
He sits at his loom in the elm's skeleton,
Looses his lacy note into the night's drift.
He is not taken in: he remembers older deceptions.

I await more information. There is none.
Silence gapes like an eclipse.
The tall dusk creaks.
Love, wild-eyed, gazes down,
Plots his galaxies

HIGH ON HYDROGEN AT THE BLUE DEMON'S PALACE

Why am I so light?
I had not thought it possible!
Light as a looped leaf, a love-child,
A May mirror

The gifts thicken: a silver ribbon
An amber wing.
June brings a ladder of petals,
The nymph-fly climbs it
To the spider's rainbow;
The poisons grip,
His soft sleep flows.

Somehow I can let go,
The torn rags mesh.
I am a rare metal,
A new blue blade, lethal.
The teeth rip and slacken.
The acids lose interest:
I am not what they bargained for.

Now the mutations quicken:
A dolphin tail, a brief orchid;
I ascend. I am ballooning,
A black spire slips past;
Now I am vapour,
Livid water, a singing isotope.
The sun stirs infinitely below;
I am its loopy brother,

A schizoid salamander,
A white star with a death-wish.
There is no stopping this balloon
My breath flashes down
The Earth is gone, a pinprick
All its daft hats, its noisy tricks!

I am high as hydrogen
I lie in the stellar wind
At a million centigrade –
Too hot even for time.

I am almost born:
A memory of leaves;
My tears fly
They stretch into blue blindness.
Gone:
An unthinkable axle

NEW MOON

A horizon as wide as an Age
The sky polished smooth as blued steel

A wash of pink over the pines
A crow leans in an Elm, like an ink-blot

The plough has passed like a pointing ghost
Leaving a wake of black spirals

The first mists weave down, curling into shadow
Everything balances

Somewhere there is a movement
A thin crack opens, the merest sliver

An invisible wire, a thread of fear sings.
I have touched something endless. I am cold.

Then, out of nowhere, a white fish
Leaps up the sky, hangs gleaming

My heart beats.
The stars wink on, a violet fulcrum

STREETS IN KEIGHLEY

All the way up from
Oak Grove, Elm Grove, Apple Street
Pear Street, Bocking
to Halifax Road, they say
come in under the shadow
of my shining brass door-knockers
and I will give you
beads, buttons, lace, muslin,
velvet, loose-strife, and
black Withens water.

He says
'you'd best stick to t'road –
nothing up here but
sheep's bones and sheep's wailing'
and thuds back up the cinder path
to his rows of useless,
wind-lashed cabbages

SHAMAN

for John Agard

Is this the way
dawn comes in your country?
A hushed leaning,
a breathing-out
of forgotten gods?

With your snake eyes
your hands flicking
like knotted lightning
you conjure
the single shy flower
out of our deserts.

With your raven voice
your panther silence
you sing back the green
ghosts from the childhood
we have banished.

Poetry is a word for it.
We have not looked, but
there is something new
suddenly in this room
standing with us –

soul, nakedness, our
severed knowledge.
Tonight in Brixton

they are burning, maiming,
looting for lack of it.

In Iran now, petrol
bombs bloom orange
over ruins that were once
its oracle;
all our history has come down
to this:

heart, without you
our world is narrower
and more lethal
than a knife point:
there must be no more shrinking.

Going home beneath
icy stars I pray
snake, raven, panther,
river of steep shadow
do not desert us

AFTER THE ICE

Black earth and straw, sodden
in a deep swathe
inlaid with the tractor's
unwavering ladder.
Dew swells, glistens on hawthorn.

After weeks of shiftwork,
the wind rests; lambs balance, wet-
voiced behind hedges, and fall
like a drift of tissue. Fields
warily free themselves of armour.

At home, the Irish linen teacloth
Blu-tacked to the wall
dances with its Disney-load
of vetch, yellow-wort, quince
and self-heal;

but 'nobody comes', you complain.
One by one you've
scared them all off:
friends, relations, neighbours,
window-cleaners, deliverymen.

Uncle Jack, informed
one afternoon his politics
and laughter were too loud;
Aunt Rose, who stopped
'popping by' after fifteen years

because you'd had words
over Uncle George's antique dresser;
Archie next door, who, last summer,
slipped out before dawn
to move his onions a foot
onto our land, out of 'pure

unprovoked malice'.
And Uncle Ben, the champion racer
on his last, squealing visit
sat in the kitchen in shorts,

dropped fat from his beef
sandwiches, and *sweated*.
They're all going down
into the slime-dark
sea of faithless, smooth-talking shif-

ty-eyed beer drinkers
leaving you speechless
with no recourse but the past.
Alone, in the television light,
your collection of miniatures

glows with fugitive colour:
Cognac, Peach brandy, Crème de Menthe,
Cointreau – potions you'll never
drink now, or move from their
allotted, dustless spheres.

At the last, my rapt
hieratic moment fails.
I must lie down, Yeats
whispers, where all
the ladders start.

I take the back path
snaking through bracken
and silver birch, to a hollow
of bramble, compressed
leaf-mould and moss, my breath

drowning the world's lyric
and incantation;
poetry seems at best
uncalled for,
at worst impotent. Alone

I count my losses: evasion,
indifference, guilt,
animosity, fear;
all familiar ghosts, compounded
lapses of humanity –

and consider the scapegoats:
all the media trash,
greed, poverty, overpopulation,
crime;
but it won't wash.

I'm present in this moment's
glistening sphere.
The world's patterned
for our freedom;
the ladders start here

AQUAE SULIS

Always somewhere there's a man
in a torn mack
going quietly downhill
with a bad cold, a slow puncture

an out of date map
and 10p short of the train fare.
Always there's a thin man in a bar
who hasn't slept for two nights

and can't make out what town he's in
but when the time comes god damn it he'll
go down fighting.
And when the gloom is inhabited only

by the slack syntax of a laid-back cabbie
he weaves over to you and rasps
*guess there's someplace this all makes sense
but sure as hell we ain't head'n' there.*

Usually there's a badly-tuned radio
balanced on a window ledge
playing Dylan, or *let the good times roll,*
the words slugged senseless by traffic.

Towards dawn there's a clean half-moon
touching the spires
while a man dreaming in a distant room
cries out for more dishcloths.

And in Queens Square a down-and-out
gropes for pockets which always elude him
with fingers that will not feel
for a lighter that never worked anyway

CLEMATIS

It goes out of her head the moment
she thinks of it;
she wanders from room to room trying

to work out what to cook for tea;
she loses her red box
of thread and darning needles.

She remembers the shine
on the crushed velvet
she embroidered for her first dance

but what the man said yesterday
about the fused washing machine
is beyond her.

She watches the blackbirds feed:
her horizon is the two-foot lattice fence
laced with birch light.

She rests; the lifelong snubs
of words like taxi, cocktail, theatre,
garage, are fading out; she's rising

above them, a dark-haired figure
slipping nightly through the grass
to her woody shrine:

a trickle of spring
water, leaf-mould, clematis –
a few veined stars quivering

AZALEAS AT KEW

'and between every two moments
stands a daughter of Beulah.'
WILLIAM BLAKE

Strayed acrobats in limp lilac
tented
over damp sawdust.

Nothing left us but
draw on silence,
wait for the descant

to rise out of dusk
welding sense to dream
till what we came for

flares incandescent
in the taut space between
one thought-span

and the next. 'No Susan,
Rhododendrons
are bigger, and don't smell!'

The glassy lady
teachers forward
across fly-by-night puddles:

'Come along now. No time
to dawdle.'
The scene lost.

Spool back, play it again.
But the brain's held
nothing, save truculent rain

scouring the grass.
Days are numbered
once more. We'll move house,

post letters,
take last-minute breaks
abroad, and winter quietly

in a small border town
where the trapeze-girl
will haunt us nightlong,

looping through lime-light
over an undertow
of glowing emerald

FLATLANDERS

They're all do-it-yourselfers.
If it moves, nail it.
If it cracks, slap Polyfilla
in it before teatime
or the devil will sail through
sure as daylight.

A garage crammed with clamps,
oil heaters, gears, glue
and worn chisels in rows
waiting for resurrection.
Next door's lawn clipped
to a tolerance of plus or minus
three millimetres.

They say: never laugh when
the wind's in the east.
Never look a gift horse in the mouth.
Never trust a man whose eyebrows meet.
Never call a kettle black.

They've seen the last of the gods
hounded from the hills by pipes,
pumps, pylons, switching stations
and TV masts; heard the stream
at the bottom of the wood panting,
reduced to skin and bone
and a glitter of fox fur.

the women sit solid each evening
staring the sky down, thinking
how many summers since dusk
grew big with wild
vermilion within them?

The men take the *Telegraph*,
tie back the roses carefully with green twine,
commiserate at street ends,
never say die,
know what's good for them

BEECHES IN JULY

as if the sun had poured itself through
yet another glass, and forgot to say when

as if time had suddenly clicked
that it was no longer needed, and clocked off for good

as if space had gone off to have a ball
and couldn't find its way back in time

as if trees had been given carte blanche
to say anything they pleased, and found themselves speechless

as if seeds had been taught the wrong algebra
and were turning out acres of unusable angels

as if words had caught their own reflection
in the silence, and turned pale as paper

as if music had discovered it didn't need sound
and could play all its notes at once

as if the wind had been caught red-handed picking
all love's locks, and fled the country in a panic

as if death had been given its cards on the spot
for falling asleep on the job this single second

INTERREGNUM

I am among ruins.
I am in the dead
place between places,
the wilderness of burnt ladders.

Feeling is a minimal
whitening, a shrunk head
almost missed
at the wood's border.

The path will not lead
forward, but again and again loops
back to this clogged lake
I passed long since.

I don't know what I lack
but I can't leave:
the earth is a blind ball of need
which won't be soothed;

I must return,
set down the sack of the will,
attend to what was scorned;
I bow down at the invisible

gate, and let the faint dancer
who knits the dead
edges of the year
begin his dance

HOUGHTON MILL

All night we sleep with the song of the deep-wheeling water.
Now dawn speaks, frost-tongued, across the white levels.
Swift wings ascend the race like a gift of laughter.

The risen sun rakes the shafts of tooled bevels
Telling the long secrets of the glides
Etching with flakes of gold the flanks of the blind wells.

What webs, what skeins of green spider the stopped tides!
What dappled rust on the slats of the oak rims!
What rubies in the glades where the dun seed rides!

But already it fades, dips, slips, sways and dims
Into a glass-faced, guttering space
Gaping with laths, lattices and limbs,

An anachronism, a tottering edifice
Its bolts, beams, stays, rafters rotted through
Its cataract tamed to a toy, a trickling moss –

Though golds, greys, ochres, reds and cobalt blue
Hold fast, fierce and furious as a snake's spite
Fused in a fallen, fleeting axle – it will go,

Fade slow, half-noticed among the slick lights
Into a spell, a shell of lost purposes, a housing
For patched tramps, lovers, and cats

A husk of stems, shafts, twists, half-echoings
Where the proved rule palls, the sure rhythms falter.
As the last lamp fails, the wind moves over its long loanings

THE BEACH CAFÉ, ABERGELE

Today she hasn't bothered to take down the shutters.
Veneered bricks peel from squat walls;
outside, on puddled concrete, a single square
table, red against black. The vanilla slice
I'm trying to eat breaks into dust.
Sparrows terrorize each other for crumbs.

The sugar bowl is spattered with heavy raindrops.
on the beach a rusting coca-
cola tin vanishing in sand.

As I leave, the small scene fixes
to a splash of reds and greys,
a grainy print already turning to history.
Again, something has quietly evaded me:
the long nights are queuing up ahead, promising
closed curtains and Clint Eastwood repeats.

A motorcycle speeds past,
a shock of wet chrome
melts in a squall of seagulls

IN MEMORY OF THE SIXTIES

The paisley curtain
had just proclaimed itself
emperor of the universe
and was already banning gravity

and the principle of equivalence;
rainbow trout were dancing
along the electric keyboard
practising twelve-tone scales

while the pencils we'd been using
to capture it all
had become polaris missiles
and were sharpening themselves

for immediate deployment.
It was at this precise moment
I decided this would be my very last
chocolate mousse

IN MEMORIAM VANGISA

died 1981

Whose angels were fire
and the wandering goat-faced wind of October

Whose delight was the furious dialectic
of tramps and post office assistants
cornered in the innocent-eyed morning

Who railed against the tyranny of the opaque word
dropped like lead into the liquid evening

Whose forked laughter blossomed like pentecostal fire
over the neighbouring gardens
shrivelling the wooden gnomes to ash

Who considered the intimate workings of dead pigeons
and the ministry of education
with a nice impartiality

Who was finally victorious over electric toasters,
bed linen and VAT returns
having consigned them all to the ignominy of the conditioned

Who watched the seasons come in over his years
tattered and bowed,
like a procession of limping clowns

Who saw lilac nuzzling the window pane in spring
cloaked like a sad priest offering solutions

Who felt the love of wife and children
like a long howl of nakedness in the dark of winter

Who came in out of the flesh of his life's storm
and found a slow death of days in lobotomized wards

Who abandoned at last the cracked consonant
and well-oiled vowel
for the wind-howl and the black raven's lament

Whose flesh at death became bright limestone
fathering from its heights generations of proud forests

GOING HOME

Again you tell it:
how at five, you were not allowed
to go to the flashy brick school
on the summit of Butcher Brow,
because the rain
made the domed cobbles lethal.

Instead, you trailed
to the squat Catholic shed
on Chorley Road, and at home-time
endured the slagging of the yobs
skiving from the state school
out of reach in its sly wilderness;

and how in July
you couldn't afford the seaside
and made do with a tent
of borrowed curtain fretted with mildew
thrown over a pole on the shy margin
of the allotments;

Something in you called
for recompense. Across sixty years
you kept faith. Now, in a new estate
on the rim of a dour village
whose shortweight soil sinks
half a foot before meeting the snubs

of flint, clinker and slate;
wind-wracked and ringed with beech,
avenues of hard-nosed businessmen
and a swart, penny-pinching
butcher from Rochdale –
you stand each morning among

heights of willowherb,
damp parapets of blackberry
harebell, and scarred valerian –
hearing hillwater seep
like a quiet scalpel through mud,
and sea birds skittering,

your shy green eyes
alert for the fitful sun glint
in fragments of glass
(pocketed years ago
on a Coronation outing to Hull)
now fallen among

cracked Jubilee plates
and a clogged watering can,
patient as the broken trove
in the clint – Alpine Violet,
Cornelian, Corallite, and sly
cloudy Obsidian

UNCLE JOE

Years ago, everyone had one –
tattered black blazer
leather-edged pockets worn to a shine
old corduroys from way back, silver-
tipped pipe always overflowing
onto the lace chair arms;

emerged nominally intact from a campaign
he never talks about
but was caught exposing himself
outside the railings of an infants school
in his hometown, and spent some months
in a discreet residence for jiggered citizens

generally rolls up around midday
just as the roast's going in
and tells you the story you know backwards
of the secret teaching he got
from a holy man in Tripoli, in exchange
for some timely advice about zinc.

Hints he knows something you don't
about Aunt Mabel's will
but always hazily changes the subject
at the first sign of interest;
is on a very strict diet on account
of the old legacy from his Burma days

but while you're on the phone he
gets remarkably quickly through
two chocolate eclairs and a jam doughnut
without any embarrassing side-effects.
Has a battered watch, its silver
worn to the brass with ceaseless pocketing

permanently stalled at five past two –
the hour it stopped a sniper's bullet
in Aqaba or Jedda.
Shows you for the tenth time
the stained book bound in half-sheep
got from a shady trader in the Gulf:

'See this – rare edition of the Koran –
Old Persian – inscribed by an intimate of the Sultan
about 1250.'
You haven't the heart to tell him
it's a modern Arabic-Dutch dictionary
useful only for propping wonky writing desks

Once in, you could never get rid of him
till one day, pipeless and hatless
he heaved out
through an open door into a raw nor'wester
and that was the last of him
anybody ever saw or heard

he pops up occasionally in dreams
as a tattered tom limping along area walls
at dawn, with something red and squirming
in its jaws; you know secretly what he's after
but you could never allow it, with his history –
not in a million years.

if you haven't got an uncle joe
you'd be well advised to place a discreet small ad
in the Times, or maybe the Tatler;
but keep an eye out for fakes: thousands
of uncle joes were turned out in the seventies
by the more opportunistic poetry mags.

if you're interested, I can tell you
the way to distinguish
a fake from an original is this:
fake uncle joes often walk out on a calm day
after a short nap in the sun –
and take their pipes *with* them

ALL THE WAY DOWN

Webbed bloom of used blackberries
Spiders hanging over
Nothing
Oak leaves abandoned in heaps
Like an impossible jigsaw
Roses are pared to crepe skulls
Stooped in ground-mist
The earth still as last month's *Gazette*
Mildewed among cabbage stalks

You cradle the wet corollas
Of turnip-rind in both hands
All the way down
To the compost's mossed settle.
Fine rain feathers through the beeches
On a single held note,
A long sanctus, sensed
Somewhere below the threshold

JUST LIKE OLD TIMES

I'm just off the 54 bus from Croydon.
It doesn't look much like a city any more
more like the waste-plot

a circus has just moved on from.
Over the bridge, big foreign graffiti
curl like fat

caterpillars.
A brown mangy moon, going
at the edges,

lurks behind Beckenham Cemetery.
In the sodium dark beyond the spikes
there's something playing

hide and seek with itself
among rusted hair sprays and
smashed wing mirrors.

In your road, blue irises are
over the moon, making Miro eyes
at each other, choc-a-bloc in their

chocolate box rockeries.
From every gaping window, a squall
of disgruntled babies

being levered into sleep. Your bedroom light's on as I snib the gate.
It's tropical: a flamingo-

tinted bulb in a coolie lampshade
from Habitat; cataracts
of spider plants purl

from steamy terraces of white
pine bookshelves;
my plaster alligator still snoozes

with his sellotaped leg
among the carefully dusted swamps
of plate-glass and bamboo

and a kitsch sand picture from Guernsey
which gets stuck halfway
through its indigo sunset.

We chat about pollution
and the sick rain-
forests, and how it's probably

already too late. I wonder
if we're both beginning to tip
over the hill

and having a last stab before
gliding down into geraniums,
evening classes on the post-modernist

novel, and seventies nostalgia.
In bed, I try to read a new Iris
Murdoch, but something keeps

dropping off. About midnight
the late Matisse duvet dis-
appears over the edge. I grope

for it, but give up half way
thinking isn't this
just like old times? Except

I don't believe there's a cottage-
pie in the sky any more,
though I search

for hours, all the way back
over your cool
moonlit pelvis

part three   1986–98

POPPY

For love, say, this solitary watcher
parachuted into summer's climax
a red nebula flickering at a field's edge
insistently radiating a single clear wave,
as if time were running out
and everything depended on this one colour
somehow getting through

as a healer, seeing the waste,
the deepening turmoil
might come at evening, unexpectedly,
and from decaying shelves unearth
his last smouldering remedy
and set to work, circled by curious eyes
without fuss, or needless questioning

THE FIRING

A moth tumbles
to its moment
of wreckage.

A world thought-derelict:
thistles stopped
in their seed-clouds;
stubble sky-
stunned,

the raked shell
of a tractor
stalled, glittering.

Gulled fields
blab straw and smoke:
a land leaping
vermilion, as if galled
by the moon's creepage.

a country with no
exits, but groves
we are goaled in, by

moth dust, leaf
scum, wing
shiver

HAWORTH

Grey ash.
Hills splashed with scarlet.
Rain, like a tear-stained face
at a darkened window.
And the telegraph wires
stretching into space
without end

NEW AGE

Before we get stuck in
I'd like to say
just a few words about the course.
This is the team.
We are here to help you grow
not batter you into the ground.
It will be helpful to remember this
when the ugly face of doubt
arises, as it surely will.
We are sure you will quickly get used
to the silence and the damp
and even find them beneficial.
To help you settle
there are duvets, flowers in vases,
hot showers, recycled toilet
rolls, and endless quantities
of organic soya milk.

There is no need to shudder
on hearing a bell: it is only there
to help you share
your sense of group responsibility.
We do ask however that you be punctual
for the work periods,
not take showers before five a.m.
or talk to the sheep
until lunch is over.

We would also request
that you do not mix with the locals
who are given to gossip
and have an uncooperative approach
to the concept of radical growth.

This is the meditation room.
We'll be spending quite a bit of time
here, so we keep it a touch
on the cool side, so you won't get
sleepy, in which event
we have some interesting ways
of keeping you in contact
with your essential earth energy.

Remember this is not an assault course:
Clarity, Rootedness
and Positive Acceptance
are the qualities we're looking for.
And remember the vast majority
of those who come here
survive, though rarely return
to a normal lifestyle.

However, meditation does change you
and resistance, as we all know
means lack of receptivity
to the communal energy.
So we do strongly encourage you
not to attempt to leave
during group sharing

devotional ceremonies
or any other activity.

This is the interview room.
I'm sorry it's a bit
on the small side.
Don't be put off by my
taking discreet notes
while you talk: I can assure you
that those who maintain
a positive attitude to our instruction
and take the work periods seriously
have nothing at all to fear.

This is the Tree Pose:
we'll be doing quite a bit
of this one. Your foot
should be pressed evenly
into the groin, keeping the trunk
erect, the buttocks soft
and letting your belly flop out
quite freely if it wants to.
The pain will be only temporary.
If you find you keep falling over
this is simply because
you are not a tree. Yet.
Radical growth takes time.
Our philosophy teaches that,
given an attitude of positive
acceptance, really the sky
is the limit.

Finally, from Sunday onwards
showers will be taken outside
in the plantation, and we
will be changing over
to an exclusive diet of nutrient-rich,
biologically balanced pond water.
We trust that you will
enjoy your new lifestyle

BARDO

Woken, the first morning
by hierarchies of owls
and the long Os
of the firs in their taut fastness;
The night before, I'd dug
a wedge of grey

slate from an elm bole,
drawn by its web
of faint markings, and hushed
sea-tracery. Now it stood
in a lit space as the sky unwound
a skein of absolute turquoise

over the roof's scarred chisel,
lawns stunned
with frost, and ice-caps stark
as starfish in derelict jam jars.
Sounds came, crisp and perfect
as Christmas money: a jeep

bringing hay to cows
anchored in cold;
the tooled precision of the electric
clock humped over the Rayburn.
Moments microscoped
over breakfast: the half-squeak

of window stays; an apple
being cleaned and quartered,

the pale core-prism turning
to ochre on the beaded plate.
Then the suck
and slither of paint over lapsed

stonework, a power cable swinging,
its opened socket
a squeal of newborn colours.
For an hour the half-
forked patch by the oak
is brilliant with trilled ovals

(where two years back
damsons were lying, nosing earth
like blind, urgent animals)
Then dusk, a frayed
smoke-mask slumped
at the boundary hedge; paths

ebbing into darkness,
a warp of impossible choices:
the new moon
clowning across the horizon
bringing unavoidable knowledge
of shrugged reaches, dereliction

of beauty. *On the second day*
you will see the soft, smoky light
of the hell realms
and you will be drawn by it....
The slate patterns with rain
as I carry it

with its dulled eye of lichen
to the shrine, place it among
flickering porcelain
and a mob of shadows;
OM TARE swirls and rises over
the cows still unmoving

in the fields; I remember
the farm-hand's cry, far off
in the stiff half-light:
a green syllable
gliding without effort over the pines,
catching the sunrise

MEETING MY FATHER AT
HOUGHTON MILL

It's almost dark as you arrive,
the heavy paragraphs dropping soundlessly
over cool mustard fields.
River mists curl, trout
gulp towards the alien surface.

You seem smaller here: more vulnerable;
your sight is worse: it's a struggle to read the
sign over the cycle shed.
At the stairhead you hover, calling –
a grey-white bird unable to roost.

All around the stacked machinery rusts.
The low moon scribbles on the wall
with her last stub, but you
notice nothing, puzzle over the mill-
stones, continue with your tea.

I cannot read your world: it shrinks
from me as the night spreads
like spilled ink across your sentences.
Through till dawn I hear your voice searching
alone and weightless

with its single, stressed syllable:
Where? Where?

ANGELS

The midnight bulletins shriek
with car-crime, credit-crunch,
ram-raids and semtex,
but none of this interests me:

what I'm primed for are the gaffes:
an abandoned Intercity
plastic food tray,
scribbled-on napkin or

a hastily crumpled Twix wrapper.
I scrutinize timetables for
inconsistencies, notes added
in a different typeface.

A rucksack spiked with tackle
and blue nylon, or a fire
in someone's back garden
are dead givaways.

It's a long shot but
I've waited too long to admit
they may never show.
I take long hikes at dusk,

avoid the made-up road,
note stones in the path
getting whiter as the day fails.
I hear the phone wires whirr

in the wind, the soft chirp
of answering branches.
Now I see the pale
shapes I called angels.

They look awful.
They say they've blown it,
they're all washed up, and I'm
the only one left who can help

RELATIONSHIP

We're at a place where two
skeltering spills of water
surprise each other on moss
then freefall

to a sullen, lichened pool.
Most of the time we're silent;
when we speak it's to name
species of trees, animal tracks,

point out the tenderness of leaves.
There's no wind, just
a brilliant star
which we carefully ignore.

At night we place a sword
of faint knowledge between us
hoping it will hold the flood
long enough for some pale root

to find its balance and take hold

DEFINITELY NOT A
WHYTE & MACKAY DAY

Sheep lurch
and clatter up the cobbles
crying *don't speak to us,*
everything's ruined

and it's all
your fault. The black-capped
nor'easter says *must try*
harder and spatters

the tarmac
with huge ink
blots and before I can say
grey rabbits

the morning's
a lifetime away,
a picture postcard in stunning
colours, saying *it's*

all just
as you remember it,
lots more to say,
wish you were here

WORDSWORTH AND
THAT SORT OF THING

Christmas in Cornwall

Water. Gulls. Astounding views.
Great vessels of many nations.
Coy stone steps skip skyward,
misting into lilacs.
Everything to shout about.
But I can't.

I hunger through thickets, lust
thigh-deep in brambles,
am granted Sights:
a stranded basking-shark (sans head)
stripped and shredded by crows
and worse: a sheep's fuselage, derelict
skull wrecked in a fence,
overcoat half-on, its last panic freeze-
framed for truer seeing;
a cliff of pink
strata crimped like brain tissue;

the 'Man O' War' saloon: tinsel flames,
a canned demented choir,
and terminal diners in bibs and paper hats.
I cry 'spirit, enough!'

The Eddystone flickers;
Christmastide bells claw
across the slack;

lanterns and snowmen
swing behind windows; still
the thing needful mews
and wails somewhere, stunned
bloodied and unreachable.

All the way home I try to relax
while a man in the next seat
alternately whistles and recites
smutty extracts from the *Mail*
to his sleety wife.
I want now your Astounding Views,
Your many nations.
I want your clefts and softnesses.
Great Vessels. Wafted lilacs

THE BRAINFEVER BIRD

Rivers up in the air
are a bad sign
especially
when they are in flood
and loaded with starved bodies
embracing
car maintenance manuals

next will be the fire
mass consumption and
unusual darkness

everybody knows this but keeps quiet

and now this omen this
chain of bones this blood
clot alights to tell me
the refrigerators are coming
my days will be black windows
the musical attics
are all dead

WOODSPURGE

A sun-burst reveals these voyagers,
embryo magi, of all places
in this midden, rainswathe, blest
and bestial –

impossible lacework of satellite software
incongruous
as an arc welder at Claridge's –
nodding like a Tingueley joke or bug-
eyed Venusian;

unreachable leafwork like midnight geometry,
electron-spin, thought-mist,
sudden forgiveness
among virulent undergrowth

so that
on a morning like this,
the earth's lobes new-scented,
the wind song-tailed, reticent,
the close lane languid with intricate siftwork –

out of the nightmare our eyes may lift
and light
on a trace of the sealed image measured into flesh:

plangent, ephemeral, guileless, but
not impossible

AVEBURY

Fog fall: cradle and cascade
of feral gloom
seeping through
crushed strata to spill

naked to the sun feast,
anointing zenith and nadir
in a litany of excess.
Perhaps here's one place

where the arc of dawn's
not cancelled
by the sprawl of sham gold
on drenched tarmac.

Lift the cold, beaded ear
of the latch and enter
the cloud-soaked grove:
spider works lie

spiked on grass, as though
a sea somewhere
wrestled to return;
wait in the bulge of shadow

till the stones'
appalling grace ratifies
what the eager clasp
hungers for: fusion

without abdication,
possession without glut,
the unimpeachable poise
of self acceptance.

For an instant all
seems possible: the cleft
of doubt healed, mind
unclenched

from the clock's decades.
Across the meadow
headlights fret perpetually
beneath unreachable elms

OPENING

What dank god squats
in this hub, this last ditch
of moss and bogweed
where time turns
to a toil, sun to a glazed
glut of light,
an untraceable aching?

What scotched spirit
crushed to a fever
nudges back at moonfall
from the waxed lip
of the Convolvulus?

What rare planet spins
in the eye of mist
like a gift
for our awaking?

PRELUDE

I woke and heard my voice
red gash of sound
shaking to rid itself
of its birth-cord

then woke again
into a spray of light, proud
over sandstone, and the hung
vowels of bells.

Dawn, and this city waking:
impalpable heart
remaking us each moment
in its own image

CONVERSATION IN MIDWINTER

'You can't change', he says, 'nobody changes
really. You just go on
mending, patching, shoring up,
bending as the gale passes.' Yet he
believes in Marx – or did once;
the staunch brotherhood just around the
corner; massed fists, voices in unison
raised across the shop floor,
the *Daily Worker* announcing
final and glorious victory over
the capitalist claptrap.

Hates corgis, greenfly, junk
food, ITV, royalty, motorists, rock
music, and God;
argues heatedly with barmaids about
the imminent birth of the revolution, yet
is baffled into silence by the perpetual
cold war between east,
west, wealth, hunger, rest,
action. Avoids churches
save as a place to eat sandwiches
when the weather turns wet; battles
through long winter evenings with spin-
driers, stopped clocks, obstinate
bicycle gears; watches
on lengthening February days
the linked leaves rot
in their clagged anchorage
of floodwater; cannot believe

the curl and mesh of the crocus's
closed fist, as it eases through loam
to drink the moor's seepage.

'There's change everywhere,' I reply,
'you can't live without sharing
spring's confidence,
winter's bleached wreckage.'

NO SHOUTING
NO SKATEBOARDING

Whichever way you turn
they get you man.
You stand still for two seconds
they get you for unpatriotic behaviour.
And those fucking metal gates
up there ready to slam
down at a moment's notice.
Oh yes they've got everybody exactly
where they want them: just you try
shouting or skateboarding down here.

Did you notice the liftman back there
pretending to read a newspaper?
And those ventilation grilles –
TV cameras.
That red manhole
cover wasn't there yesterday
they're getting ready
don't trust the lifts, only the spiral
staircases are safe now

They're all nutcases man.
Only after midnight when
the trains have stopped you can
stand in the tunnel and whisper
clear as music, shit man,
perfect solitude, that's one thing
they can't take away.

Look at their faces
NO RUNNING NO CYCLING
blank as a death cell
I'd walk up if I were you.
See that wire mesh up there?
Twenty thousand volts
all they have to do is give a signal
I'm not joking man, I've seen it
Any day now. All nutcases

147

ZATTERE

for Angela

The tethered domes of San Salute
high over the lagoon –

heart within a heart,
memory within memory.

Somewhere, a nudge of doubt
a sullen grinding of ice-ledges.

The bells soften slowly in their mist-robes.

148

Now your solitary Bach phrases
are wafted towards me through the oleanders
with the smell of warm cedar from the Accademia.

If I speak now
a lock will be opened
I will never be able to close again.

The note swells,
ebbs away.

It is enough

TORCELLO CATHEDRAL

Trying to remember
exactly how
the lizards slanted
on their dizzy lecterns

and how shyly
the sunlight entered
the veined marble
below the altar

I can only recall
exactly how
your white slip rested
motionless against your legs

and how your fingers felt
moving small in my palm
like something
just born

TOM

Morning. Drenched parapets.
Weak sun
glinting through cloud slits,
spearing the sodden moss.
In the low-roofed kitchen you stoop,
polishing plates
with an abandoned glee
I'd give a lot for;
explaining to anyone who'll listen
the laws of human cell division,
the sperm's ascent into grace,
and how a hologram fragment
rekindled in its own birth-ray
conceives the whole brimming pattern
with nothing lost.
Over coffee you tell of Proust
tramping the night in hooded frenzy
trying to regain the track
back to the sea-washed birthplace
at the hushed rim of everything
and Rimbaud, desperate in his loft
ranting with needle and penknife.

When it's finally your turn to read
you sit with a plate in your lap
pointing the light,
the page angled like a specimen
over the instrument's lit circle,
fine-focusing on a phrase
till the meaning uncoils,

flicks into lucidity; then
throw yourself back in your chair
like an uncle with a magic sixpence
grinning, triumphant.
Your delight conjures a quick
small hand at my elbow:
I'm nine again, and up at dawn
sunk to the knees in bluebells, rapt
at the new silky webs spread everywhere
or in late July
in a hollow at the top of the wood
toes mushroom-pale among mulch
and cuckoo spit
brimming with peace.

Now, a slender flame
graces your words,
wavers, and rekindles. Outside
willows are abandoning
their useless maps.
Come, prolific veteran.
Drench me in word-light.
Stretch the warp tight
till the track shimmers,
the wound knits,
the pattern focuses

TORCELLO

'and his dark secret love does thy life destroy.' (BLAKE)

Say birth starts here:
with this weightless breath, these
sifting footprints.
I'd believe it dearly.
But the tomb of the past is the heart's
locked volume:
things understood
hardly, and too late,
loved too little
and for dumbest reasons.
I'd kick free loss given half
a moment whole,
and live shadowless.

But whole glances rarely;
here, we trace perfection
in marbled inches. I creep from Marco
Polo to Santa Croce
under sleeping troll-packs
of cumulus. Ahead
San Salute, globed molten starship,
sightless and blinding,
in stasis above
dancing silks of turquoise
and aquamarine.
A cold wound unheals
under the drone of tongues.
I tread no further.

Would it have been the same
if I'd huddled safe
in the suburbs of the terminally
sane, turned blind
from the spreading sootfall?
Mind has its miles to make,
must drag its sack of dark
through ruck, furrow and bog
whatever lassitudes lame it.
I have hope, but loss
can't be sneered down dogwise:
it springs perpetual
as wind braids lakewater
or rain rails diagonal
across slagged sky, where
Celt and Saxon howled
for a spent heath
and half a rood of shale.
In the pelting dawn
of a north Lancs mill town
my father prowls
the shop floor of his bedroom,
memory clogged with stale
newsreels: True Grit,
Tour de France winners,
Mr Chamberlain's Note;
while the sepia rose
blooms prophetically in plaster
above the picture-rail.

Memory rots; but not need:
it endures, smoulders,

flames into limbs. Fear scrapes
and tunnels, treks to far logics.
Here, despite high words
our tons of hurt
weigh us to earth. Hell's not
geographical; (even in paradise
we tooth-and-clawed a whole
Saturday morning in the Car
supermarket over my craving
for expensive Emmental).

Journeys uplift and distance, yes,
but if the seed's flawed
bring no release;
on a day-trip to the Boboli
gardens, feeding squirrels
and drinking our Earl Grey
from fat flasks we
calmly agreed sex
wasn't a problem
so long as we didn't actually
have it; though behind our eyes
if we'd cared,
a mute child moved,
paled into silence.

But the bells ring me back:
a canal's wriggling
in its shawl
of purpled limestone;
in the sun's elixir
distance ligatures;

amber goes haywire
under drugged bridges.
We're leaving the city
to echoes of boat horns homing
and engine babble
under hot varnish.
The salt shallows flicker.

At midday the prow nudges reed-
beds, fretting the sulky
scents of hibiscus
and bay; lizards quiver
on the cathedral parapet,
intense in lakes
of bronze and emerald.
Heat takes hold. A bell
stalls at its limit.
Sunlight curls the paint
on an upturned hull
at a path's end.
Pines' inflorescence
graces the day's caesura.

We're walking, finger-linked,
waist-high in heat,
watching sea-crabs
cram the inlet like lifers
crazy for news,
the lagoon's glaucous
dialect wrapping us.
A wrought gate, gashed to rust,
goes nowhere but to bees,

marshes, and born-again
Coke bottles.
How to square this upstart
joy, long-banished elf,
with the stalking incubus?

We pay a thousand lire and
visit the damned
in their racks of terrible light.
Even at this chaste zenith
everything's stained;
the trick seems to be
accepting it.
My dear, we agreed
our heaven's a mirror too bright
long to live in.
We tried. Survived. Just.

We write letters now
in rituals careful and clear:
Keep strong. Keep positive.
Pages with the pain snopaked out
and useless for singing.
I wonder often
in what immaculate cage
our child grieves.
Somewhere, in a yard-end,
from a rain-etched lintel,
in windless cat dark,
a petal, weightless as spring,
spirals down, dissolves,
begins again

STAUPS MILL

for Ken

The same voice shaking upwards for ever:
unless you become as brickdust
or as bleached cotton
you shall not enter
                    the kingdom.

Not silence
or the shrunk protest of pistons
drowned in the unthinkable riverblack;

not the rusted barrel-hoop locked
into a helpless parody of itself

or the hollyhock by the graveyard
bent double
in denial of dreaming

but somewhere in the gaps between

like the moment you sat in the axle bearing
with harebells and a handful of yarrow
and watched a long time
where rods of spring water fell
through the raped centuries

SNAPSHOT

for my father

There you are, already half-hidden
by a dead tree; second from the left
in shorts, and an old anorak
with three buttons missing.
The writing on the back says: 'me
with Tom and Mabel at Kirkby, 1943.'
The others stand together grinning,
holding up an old boot
with long laces dangling (the joke
now escapes you).
In the foreground a chipped
mug of cooling tea. The scene
evokes dashing, pastoral merriment.
Your hand firm on your hip
speaks volumes: out
for a day's spin up Pendle, back-
slapping over mugs of strong tea
in a café at Fog Bottom,
or at night tapping out snippets
of laconic verse and racy
articles for the CTC mag.
Then you weren't stumped for words:
they sped from your erect Remington
spry and shipshape
as a chippy on an annual works outing.

You were thirty-four then. No doubt
you could have been something big
in publishing or journalism; but the word
on which everything hung
escaped you, and you went on
making do, fitting in, bearing up,
typecast in a role you neither
wanted not understood.

Now, on a damp June morning
forty years later I watch you
on your stony plot of land, tying up
runner beans with bits of wire,
back rigid, hands scored,
legs thin as an ache, grey hair
bolt upright: a grim
unflinching puppet, scarred
with years of honesty in a flat,
sniggering world.

Yet, you seem content, more
or less; but your conversation now
runs slow in a mould of acid silence,
and the chipped mug stands alone,
a neglected war monument
on the sideboard's bare summit.

Something remains undone. As you
rake the cut grass I call
to you, feeling a grief
I've never known before
spread through me.

You don't respond. All
you can feel is the wind
clawing your thin anorak,
and the words that won't come,
the stopped presses roaring
mercilessly in your ears

NEW YEAR, CORNWALL

Homeless, the light;
maimed, archaic wanderer
stumbling towards us
over granite, heaped
birch boughs,
cow-haunted saltings.

Your face beside me
fragile in its domain
of sleep
flowers from the dark.

My dear, turn to me
but do not wake:
I am gored, exiled
from my life by this beast;
unable to weep, or drink
your love's clear fountain

AND JOY WHOSE HAND

And then
we walked along the sand (trying not
to get too sentimental about it because
after all it probably was the exact spot
Bogarde had pegged out
with that awful mascara running down his cheek)
and I watched you digging for the best shells
everyone had missed all summer
and I looked out to sea, imagining Othello
swaggering home
to his own do-it-yourself hell
and I thought how everything precious is woven
so fine a doubt can ruin it
and then the sun set behind the new concrete
hotel and we talked about Eurydice lost
in that terrible tunnel and how
it probably meant that Orpheus didn't trust
his feminine wisdom and so was cut
off from it and went mad and you
found some shells that looked like black masks
and we tied them all up in a red scarf
you'd bought in the market and walked
to the water bus and the mist
rose all around us and made your lips cool
and salty and the sky was like somebody
had thrown a whole box of powdered rose-lake
and amethyst up into it and it just
hung there
and I thought of Keats then
alone in his airless room the blood

getting worse and the only person he loved
gone
and I couldn't speak and the lights came on
mauve candles across the lagoon
very dim and I just
put my hand out slowly hardly daring and
you were there

HOMAGE TO JOHN BERRYMAN

Wet April iron-shod acid light unshedding
in dust and the sharp shadows of
derelict coke-cans.
How the fruit trees flourish now daily
in the soaked turf of railed estates
and rusted railways flanking the river!

My window gives on a stream
deckled with hyacinth and dock,
hawthorn greening
and galaxies of primrose
flickering through chill twilight.
Nobody comes this way
save the barn's owner
to dump cinders or gather in washing.

In memory I go back to you
in your word-riddled tumult of
three decades past;
I wonder how much you apprehended then
in your fool's lucidity,
of coming horror?
Since your end little's happened
save terror; what can't go on
goes on, gorges and multiplies,
the best minds manacled in famine,
war, wreck, epidemic, hijack,
the clattering terminal ripped
in the stark violet
of a botched incendiary.

Before me your stiffened lifeshape gropes
through pearled mist
like a blinded king.

I see your light-starved hulk
loom loveless over your folder
of stained foolscap;
I see you lamplit in the just-open diner,
dazed and daydrowned
over a drained bourbon,
questioning not why or how
but only *when* and on *which* reef
you will be stripped and foundered.
I see you at dawn, behemoth,
grounded on somebody's third-floor
apartment landing,
sun glistering
through a low frosted rectangle,
the Johnny Walker sucked
to its dregs,
chipped coffee-mug derelict
on the wine-circled pages
of a paperback life of Keats,
spilled yellow folder of dreamsongs
in spate over green linoleum,
the unslaked day waiting outside
wordless – another riddle
you'll guess too late,
another test you'll
fail furiously,
another inquisition you'll rage through
with its legions

of crass imperatives.
I see you at noon in a crisp
east-coast hotel bathroom,
chanting Blake with a hard-on
and the bird flown betimes;
I see you slamming home the blinds
against the downward hammering
light your life squirmed under,
one eye cocked to sense
where loathing, white-hot, will lance
next weakness through.

The picture shatters;
you're a shadow, a fond fury
stalking me; the storms in moments
scathe us beyond remembering;
But here I feel almost your stained
fingers crossed in mine
as I stand, likewise unhanded
by worlds I, wilder, wished for.
I lose count of days
grounded in doubt; history's doggerel
pounds in me, and palls;
Nothing's here but dread
of myself; *of course*
I do well the jobs set me.
But they give no peace.
An inward voice rails
against a world grown childless.
And such erosions lifelong groan,
and multiply.

All winter the ripening dream stayed.
Draughts full of the warm South,
the siren Adriatic.
Melting islands. Nurture
and love and calm acceptance.
Her letters came, laden
with Carneval confetti and oleander
from the Accademia gardens,
amber sunlight in the Piazza
lured through charmed circles
of Quattrocento rose-glass.
Whatever happens, we will be together....
Words conceived in love
stiffen and glaze,
grieve into monuments.
Dreams fold, journeys telescope
to vague terraces
glimpsed between conversations.
The failed year broods in me,
lodges in the blank between breaths;
my heart shallows, ingrows,
winters in a bleak suburb,
endures,
is dumb;

        yet

something is in love
that lulls time and melts space
to a skullswidth; Keats knew:
already with thee
spelling off the encroaching hunch
of cold at his breath's core,

though not lightly;
sunlight strays, veers, dances
in midstream, daring us;
the errant scent of mustard
sun-drifted over a low wall;
a snatch of *Winterreise*
or an unscheduled Beethoven cavatina
conduces to something
not quite containable
in words' trim nets.

And against these, the furies:
adolescent posturing before chic
female students on a west-coast campus;
self-disgust, scandals, lassitude,
boredom; a man *older, sick*
and miserable-chaotic.
Missa Bones, yo' can only sing yo' own song
an' that's a fact;
take Henry's deep advice:
no one's philosophy ain't worth
a horse's toss
if it ain't lived in.
But no song homes
till the nerve's riddled
with strong knowledge. Until then:
Write as short as you can, in order,
of what matters.
The world's unending anguish
to be healed.
A son nurtured and educated.
A family increasingly dependent

on a proud and hounded poet's
capricious paycheck.
Temperance, order, self-analysis,
livelihood....

Yet the radiance when right, invisible,
sends words reckless ringing through
whole or sheared. The gash
in your pride nothing then!
The damp puppystruggle
with a torn verb, juggle of syntax,
or spouting of morning's
crisp commonplaces over
a spilt infinity of breakfast!
Then fire, fatherly, lights your signatures!
Roars unquenchable! *All right!*
You count fifty, then
I'm coming after you!
Shrieks along cindered paths.
Gagged laughter in cobwebbed
attics. You resound, wealth of angels! –
through the still-shrouded alleys;
words build and break,
shed their scents. Early sun
lagged in wan light
shakes out increments
of far flowerings.

'He took the bus to the university,
and walked onto the west end
of the Washington Avenue Bridge,
high over the Mississippi.

He jumped up onto the railing,
sat down and quickly leaned
forward. He never looked
back at all.'

Disowned fragments. Acid
blanks in the brain.
Something tugging
from a scorned darkness,
mute, unprovisioned.
How, in the end, everything
pointed to it. The drink,
womanizing, self-immolation,
guilt. How it was almost essential,
the pattern of a certain kind
of life. Part of an age:
the century's implacable logic.
In the night a frantic squall
of wings against glass,
a bird whose colours
I can only guess at,
trapped in the rafters.
I open the window, stare
a moment, hobble back
to glistenings of uncertain sleep.

Winter harbours gold;
the moon labours
over mountains,
shouldering cloud.
At last it all goes.
The horror of unlove. Decay

170

in the deep places.
Abandoning's the hardest task.
Few achieve it. Mostly it's just
indifference.
Not the poet though. He's the real
thing. What you say to that,
Mr Bones?

*(The quotation on pp. 169–70 is taken from
'The Life of John Berryman' by John Haffenden)*

TIANANMEN

No. They can't do that. It's not possible!
Even governments. It'd be suicide.
Must be a mistake. Birds meshed in the radar,
fuddled computers. But wait, this was *live*,
there were bullets on the tarmac. They were real.

And journalists. Girls in shorts, t-shirts,
flip-flops. Couples holding hands.
It was hot. People were singing.
Thus a Peking poet who was there,
in shock, but certainly not dreaming.

Britain 'deplored the massacre'. Of course.
But naturally drew the line at embargoes.
Russia belched a pompous
'now is not the time for unconsidered conclusions.'
The Japs said it was none of their business.

Once more it seems left to the poets.
Yet, if I'd been there, would I have stayed
with the crushed children, screaming mothers,
the arms with no hands,
to bring home the sick news? Maybe not.

But it's changed me. At least now
I'm clearer about what's
possible, and what isn't. And what our lot
might do if the stakes were high enough.
And where the pale stands

AFTERMATH

There's a point when the rhetoric
of governments – anywhere – must be seen squarely:
a vehicle of power and fear.
Yet year after year the educated assent,
even welcome it. As if, while there's
a voice up front spouting the same safe, slick

platitudes, it's fine by us. That threadbare
old English middle-class claptrap
runs deep: it could never happen here....
Or if it did, somehow, right would prevail,
we don't actually have to change. God's still
hugging the reins, inscrutable, somewhere.

Peking, second of June: the hunger-strikers say
class war's obsolete; we must learn from the past,
tolerate, convince by arguments.
Only that way we escape history's inferno.
Then, 2 a.m. Sunday, the unthinkable's here:
bullets, gas, tanks, clubs, crushed infants.

And may we have your response, Mr Poet?
Yes – fear. I'm alone
with no safety net; barriers are gone:
Moscow, Wapping, Peterloo, Tiananmen.
It's with us now, only, so far
with our consent – and (just) legal

FEAR

Fear, that's the heart of it.
Where all the dripping, vertiginous ladders
start. Suffering's foul taproot.
I want only, in my cynic garb, out.
Never – this above all – to snakeride
back to that seething lake.

If one small thing's been learned,
this time, surely it's that:
fire, reaching the quick
pares desire with footless alacrity.
Commend love I can't, in this
smould'ring circle. But neither

can I hole up in a thatched
deva-realm for the rest of my natural.
Mr Bones, you faced this crux hard
each dry sunrise, and still
couldn't crack it. I'm reluctant
having groped this far

to blow it now, 'specially after paying
so much for your fine first editions.
That grates.
But I fear failure. Each time shows
more of it to feed despair.
Now not stirring it up

seems wisdom. But there's something
fluttering there, deeper and uglier:
reaching a stale age with this
still unlicked. A consummation
devoutly not to be stomached.
But this at least's certain:

love can't be buried, camouflaged,
shelved, shipped abroad
or crated ladderless
in an obliging friend's attic;
evaded, feared or scorned, it's
(as Henry costly discovered) crucial

'THE CARE & FEEDING
OF LONG POEMS'

for John Berryman

Yes, I can see how the whole sad mess
could be blamed on sex (the opposite)
and what having it meant: two marriages,
umpteen affaires
not counting mirages and postprandial fumblings.
But then (as you'd doubtless say) what are friendships

for, if not to occasion blessedness:
the lights and shades that lead (on a good day)
to poetry? Ah! That's the question
that brings the men
in long white coats running over the campuses.
I'm tempted to abstain on that one too,

or, along with Tu Fu, complain that company's
an impediment to the making of good verse,
preferring herons, azalea blooms, and ice-
cold mountain water
to an August evening haggled dry
in debate or dalliance. But (as Confucius

said) t'world's a rum place;
friends, with the right touch, can bring things home
that would take a lifetime or more to dawn
in solitude;
and as regards the opposite, let's admit
that silence after long sex seems the grail

every post-Ginsbergian poet's after. But – it fades,
it fades, and is replaced by overdrafts, tax-
returns, jealousies, and interminable evenings
of Sky Channel.
And if that's ruled out, what's left?
You roamed your jagged life for that, edge to edge,

not realizing perhaps until that last bridge
it was a species not invented yet: a mate
sensitive, loyal, without judgement; someone
who knew the score
but wouldn't be dragged down – an angel even,
fog-winged and bleeding from the tumultuous future

177

EVEN THE ANT ...

'It's not easy being creative when you've got
two kids – you should try it.' Many thanks but
no. I'm unhinged enough as it is.
And these words that babble night after night
with no regard for whether I feel like writing them –

don't help. Still, maybe the lady has a point, Mr Poet.
I mean, all that fiddling with spondees
and irregular feet can't be healthy
now can it? Maybe you should, well,
go forth and multiply, a bit.

Objections crowd. In truckloads.
What if I don't ... What if it should ...
What if I forget to ...
And how should I ... and aren't there already
more than enough of the little sods?

Perhaps it's just this spring business again.
Even the trees are at it. It gets to you
eventually, even with double
glazing and extra-thick underpants.
And where would literature be now

if Joe Shakespeare had got it into his head
to take the cloth? In trouble,
that's where. Not to mention Tolstoy and the Lawrences.
Well, thank you very much. Could we
have the next question, please?

GEOGRAPHY

No doubt neurotic and largely destructive of
our mutual future is this
continual historical fingering. Two years
nearly now of debris rusting between us –
our east & west unbreached,
your cards from Leningrad and Venice
minimal & polite: love-
proof windows frosted with dead news.

Nine out of ten for protocol. But how's
this risen, I move to ask? Unlived
lives slide apart; whole countries in us now
unsayable. I don't absolve
from weakness – far from it;
there's something here starved,
bloody & grieving; but (here's a deep but):
where to dig strength, without

your love's edge to lend heart?
You took it; I failed – hard.
The dream wrecked.
Soon now wakes winter's hurl again.
Hills harbour me: I can no magic dance
make: only goad a new tense out of this
continuous imperfect:
stumbling, sullen, graceless – but sane

RETREAT

'I can deal with everything but your eyes in tears.'
JOHN BERRYMAN

Hardest yet, this first month without you,
ignorant of the voices you inhabit:
anxious, carefree, desperate
or longing. And letters that find me
are already fixed, historic,

like light from galaxies: what arrives bright
and innocent, may be a lie.
Not love itself, but doubt dogs healing;
what's not a game to get approval
seems forlorn philosophy, or worse: habit.

To give what's needed, at the right time,
without strings or judgement – who, on this measure,
has loved? I abstain. But then
I recall your eyes, that long weekend
sealed with tears

and I've no choice but undress
all my words, and pack them off, sheepish
to some genteel
place of retirement – and hold you, and feel
the race of your pulse, opening, earthing me

LOVE BY NUMBERS

Longings, over and over, outrageous oh!
and unstoppable! Philosophize and they flip
frigid into fundamentalism. Moralize,
they turn into bad poetry. (And Plato
would've had all writers shipped
to Chiros for spawning such unacceptable detritus.)

Outside my window, spring's caught *in flagrante*
unzipping the laburnum. Chiff-chaffs
play snakes and ladders in the blackthorn;
helicoptering dragonflies hike their mosaics
over the furled brook. Everywhere the Earth leafs,
sparkles and scents herself wantonly.

Yet here I praise you in a stark weather
of syntax, eschewing hype; a hermit
doling out words in a singularity of cold;
I love you by numbers, who should be held
as Li Po held the full moon at rapt midnight –
legless amidst wild peonies and uproar

THE WET AFTERNOON MAN

He says black
is white.

He says the fear
in the atmosphere is changing
all the money in the banks
to leather.

He shouts fuck
the Pope on Saturday afternoons
in Victoria Square
and everybody titters.

He says the more
happy little men there are
printed on the menu
the more tasteless the food.

He says the way up
and the way down are the same
that's why so many people get hurt.

He says the black
bird of loneliness is wiser
than the sour
grapes of instruction.

He says he has
a name for the police which he saves
for the really bad moments.

He says listen Mac
you can smile but
have you ever been inside a geranium?

He says if an infinite
number of monkeys were to throw
typewriters over
the white cliffs of Dover
every day for a thousand years
there'd be no bluebirds.

He says back   183
home nobody would think twice.

He says no matter
how many tigers you put
in the tank, the smile
on the face of the attendant
always amounts to nothing.

He says the food
in your mouth is always less
than the sum of its parts.

He says all the oceans
are dying of ships.

He says all those
who call a spade a spade
have never been there.

He says OK Mac,
but from now on – find your own angels

184

THE BEAST

I've decided to get rid of it. For good.
Goad it from my castle of mornings,
my riverwide evenings, my moments
of near-peace before sleep
slides in his angels of tumult.

But it won't go. It melts dull-eyed
into my thoughts' shallows.
It dares me to call it by name.
Knowing my weakness, it tosses a few
fickle, glass-hearted words, wafts

a wavering bar of birdsong. But I won't
admit it. It wants to deny me
everything. It grows fat on my longing.
It is jealous of every hope I claw at.
It doesn't care a fig.

I ignore the scent of lilac and start typing.
It thinks I've deserted it.
The morning turns uncomfortably hot.
At the open window, the first wasp
bulges, hesitates, drones towards me

185

THE PIANO

I'm tramping in bog and claggy mist
stalked by that image:
the mute woman dragged down

by the gift that was her voice,
then at the last second, cutting free.
It got to me, stirred old familiar

ghosts, shapes too close for peace:
my dad humped over a saw,
having no speech

for what was nearest,
no silence from what wheeled
always beyond reach.

And me, unable to get close
because closeness meant being seen,
picking up the tab,

cutting free.
Safer to be dumb, invisible,
bloated with blame.

Up here there's space.
Lots.
It's an element to be human in.

I'm stunned by what earth endures:
sheep locked in sheep,
stones in stone, bats in bat.

I'm grateful for this
borrowed inch of choice
that makes me me;

being able, just once, to say:
'is this where I'm at?
OK. I'll use it.'

WHAT I WANT

Something to happen, anything:
a miracle, a hurricane, a blizzard

from nowhere snuffing the roads out,
an offer of publication

over the dead phone.
I want the world to begin, or end,

I don't care which.
No, scrub that.

What I really want's
a bolt of lightning and an angel

on tip-toe with the message:
'It's finally come through

from Highest Authority:
you're OK.'

But what actually happens is
the Rayburn dies, the milk goes off,

we forget to buy the Guardian
to check for Signs of Hope

in the Middle East.
I can hear the rain lashing

the sacks of feed and netting
in the rotting barn.

I think of the ponies wintering
in a ditch up the valley, wind-scoured,

flank to flank, nostril to nostril.
All evening nothing happens,

unless you count the wine glass in my hand
miraculously emptying

MY FATHER LISTENING TO A
POETRY READING ON RADIO THREE

He sees it in *Radio Times*.
'I wouldn't mind hearing that' he says. 'They've got
nothing but snooker again on BBC.'

The first poem catches him out:
he's staring into the garden, tracking
the intense flight of a starling
from water butt to onion bed to runner beans
to carrots. He's worried about slugs.
'They completely ruined my cabbages last summer'
he says, half exasperated, half resigned
to what nature's implacable economics deal out.
He's stirring his tea. He strikes the cup
three times with the neb of his spoon to signal
it's finally fit for drinking.

The next poem's about different ways of seeing
frogs. He slops some tea on the floor,
dabs about half-heartedly with a sopping sponge.
The poem's in seven parts.
He shuffles a packet of spaghetti,
fingering its glitzy wrapping to see
what this new foreign food's really made of.
'We never buy that here' he observes
around the third stanza. 'Far too expensive.'

The last poem's about a man talking about
what making a film would do
to his sex-life were he to embark on it.

Father suddenly smacks his hands together,
barrelling his arms round his chest
with an exaggerated stage-shiver.
'That middle-un wasn't about frogs after all.
Why can't they write what they mean if they're poets?'

He cradles his tea, creaks open
the door, tries repeatedly to shut it quietly, but
fails, his mind already working out
new and terrible ways of annihilating slugs
in between snatched frames
of Steve Davis bashing the hell out of that
uppity young fellow with the hair-cut from Aberdeen

HOWARD HODGKIN'S 'RAIN' AT THE TATE GALLERY

Why this insistent
wish to kneel
where immaculate wrists
steer down
to cool among the firs' laced
sisterhood

as if an angel
were to shrink to Earth
through the perilous gate
of colour, or an exiled
king reveal his
tenderness?

THE WOUND

for Manjusvara

Where did it begin? Was it
the first glimpse,
a cool flame in a crammed
Boston takeaway, or
high over the Atlantic, caught
in the marbled afterplay of sunrise?

Maybe it begins
in the blind moment we return
to trace the lost street,
the colour we couldn't name; or
when we first jumped
from deep waterfalls

and found a music
that never dies,
never arrives, but tears us
breath by breath
into being,
into raw knowledge

VISITING YOUR STUDIO
AFTER THE FLOOD

for Varacitta

I am safe. A white corridor,
trestle-tables, art:
this is not going to alter anything.

But you drag open a drawer and salt
water sniggers out over brushes,
saucers, sellotape and used-up crimson.

Verdigris on pipes and seized hinges
makes an oiled, glistening vortex.
Huge ears of shells

loom and listen towards us;
three ravenous moons
stalk each other, deadpan

in a blue, slanting window.
They've sussed that what's going on here
is abandonment.

Up in that stained corner
is where it came from, slithering
from its nest of plaster

till it had met and married
every colour in the room.
You peel open sheets to show me

the excrescent black balloons,
the rusty explosions between faces;
unhook a flocked curtain and a slush

of amethyst breaks over crammed emptiness,
occult fans of deliquescing colour,
the sleeping blackness inside opening,

the ancient dream of rest opening,
all the torn, bloodied and disowned wings
of mercurial night opening

FISH

Your crabbed blue letters thump
down the page.
'Where are you?' they say.
'Take me home.
Take me to where I live.'
I imagine your shrunk face
at its huge window:
an extinct lighthouse
casting cold shadow
over the miles of wet sand.

You're not ready to go.
There is still some hatred unspent.
Your eye lights on
a square of fish on your plate.
*'This is what they expect me to eat. This
filth!'* You raise your fork,
stab, stab, stab, till it feels your fury.

'They're all mad here'
you write. 'Take me home.
Who am I?'

THE CALL

The loch is a grey winding library of sadness.
All the sadness we don't own ends up in it.

When we pretend to be happy the waves drift from shore
to shore like carol-singers in the falling dusk.

If we push down our loneliness its surface wells
over the blades of sedge and faded sheep tracks

like old school ink in August.
I wake in the night and hear something howling through the wind.

On the shore stands a wolf-bird with feathers of dull green fire,
unmoving, lit by its own bleak light.

It is the guardian of the books of sadness,
but there is no one left on earth who can read them

PATTI AND BILL YOUR AVON REPRESENTATIVES

The sleek lawn purring
beneath its miraculous catch of snow.
A new Chevrolet estate
cools on the gravel.

By the porch four marmalade
reindeer are stalled
under a perfect crimson heart.
The afternoon slides to the ground

and is forgotten. Shreds
of sunset become TV flicker.
I remember the dead-

eyed woman in the supermarket
padding down the aisles in slippers
clawing at packages.
Endlessly.

The matted road fades
into the woods like something
without hope.
I turn for home. I am afraid

A WALK

Holding your hand
down the steps
I feel rubbery veins
that tolerate the grope of blood,
bones that grind like icebergs.

Your face is busy
with small, furious memories:
being blamed for your sister's
romps at the Audley Range dance;
the crushed moments
of butterflies.

We're going to visit the homeless
children you know are buried
in the scabby dark
between the larches,
your eyes
slow gatherings of bleakness
staring through me into
no future

26 PIAZZA DI SPAGNA

(Keats' address in Rome,
where he died of tuberculosis in 1821)

The room is stifling and no
wider than a cupboard. Serious
girls, sleeveless in cotton
blouses and fishnet tights

caress the glass
over your deathmask; their cool
fingers read your sorrow,
yearn for a sign.

Sunlight flashes from the fountain
three flights below.
What would you not have given
to dance there also?

ROMAN GIRLS

stand edge-on to the sun
like gazelles. Know by osmosis

that they are admired
and that to be admired is everything.

are minted fresh each moment:
when they walk day begins;

when they are no longer beautiful
the world is over.

are obscure and transparent as the dark muses
of the Borghese.

are earth and fire
in one seamless equation.

Death constantly stalks them but
at the last second always misses.

The only thing lethal to them
is indifference

LEAVING OLCIO

Too early still
for the sweating chain-saw man
to gash the morning into molten ribbons.

Goats on the shadowed terraces
silent with the close memory of stars.

Green glass nested among stones
like the first note of an archaic hymn.

The edge of desire already returning
as I follow you up the track
past the store
of glowing wood-gold

THE SHOWER

for Miranda

You slip half awake
out of your last shower
and your breasts

make a little trembling dance
as you brush your hair
barefoot on the lake of marble.

I marvel at the beaker of cold
lemon water you offer me, with its
chaste spaces of cloudy opal.

Now you're hooking in your crescent
moons, to match the blouse
with its arc of sun wheels.

And somewhere there is gold,
and a song almost getting started
in the street we're leaving by:

something like tenderness, how
the spring light races and dies
over the washed squares

PLEASE REMAIN IN YOUR SEATS, WE ARE EXPERIENCING SOME TEMPORARY TURBULENCE

Really when you think, it's
anyone's guess where we'll
all fetch up: nuclear winter
most like, or melanoma,
a wind-sprayed jetty on the west

coast, the tide juggling
bleached evian bottles, or
a nine-to-five number processing
claim forms for disasters
that need never have happened

if someone had only eased up
just a fraction on the pedal.
One day somebody will
install some neat software
that tells us not to get up today,

no decisions are possible
until there is less interference,
or Saturn swims serenely into Aries.
Meanwhile the best bet is
carry on juggling

the payments, keep an eye out
for a sea change in the markets,
and try to bear in mind
what the man scribbling furiously
in the departure lounge

said, something about trust,
and luggage you must let go of,
and how each moment's the glowing end
of a thread, that goes on
out into the world, forever

MORE THAN I CAN SAY

As I pass the gate
the crackling scarlet macaw
clutching the ironwork
is a scrunched chocolate
wrapper, and the Startrek
headgear along the walls

are verses of baroque
lichen, and the whole thing's
lit by the Shadows
and flashes of Juke
Box Jury from 1960.
Then I'm out on the moor

and struggling between Jurassic
limestone throwbacks
resenting my easy mobility
and the caved-in farms
with Magicoated purple doors
are just hippie

families from Sheffield
kidding you they mean business.
Then I can't decide
whether sheep are discarded lungs
of bagpipes or worn out
bath taps

or if nasturtiums can be thruster
controls; then I wonder
if that's really not
what it's about
at the end of the day, things
standing for other things,

or perhaps I'm just trying too hard
and some buried voice
is moaning about
all that rubbishy junk you listen to.
Then it's heritage centres selling
hand-woven knick-knacks,

and franchised cafés with neon logos,
and a knot of helmeted kids
are taking the piss
outside the chip-shop,
and the Prestel
headlines are all drought

and starving economies,
and the wow-wows and bop-she-waas
are all gone under the hill,
and there's the voice again
dead on cue, saying
try telling that to the poll-tax people

NOTHING BUT A LOVE POEM

Surprises everywhere.
The gravel path from Kelvin Bridge
along the limping waters suddenly
wired off.
The sun dazzling me from three sullen
abandoned wine bottles.

Office workers bent under white fans,
already half defeated by their day.

I'm quite unable to make out
whether the plump nipples
of willow herb, or the silverhaired stars
of thistles
hold the truth
at this precise moment

TOUCH

Lest something I'd
no word for
welled alive

I never dared
touch your face,
never guessed

how feather soft
and undefended
your temple was.

Now on the pillow
it quivers
like the wild breast

of a bird
that has
flown too far

GHOST

So much of you
still tethered here:
your wholewheat
loaf, its green-grey

stars of mould just
flickering on;
a feathered
shopping-list,

your old shoes unlaced
by the back door
after your last walk.
I know now

what I most feared:
to stand alone,
the precious gift I must
not turn from.

I take the path of black
roots through the witches'
circle, follow it past
lanterns of beech

and lichen
till it turns east,
climbs, releases me
into new weather

PASSAGE

Already on this path
the sullen crimson
of your last evening
ignites, as though
all the hidden doors of your life
had snicked open at once.

The newborn shadows raise their gifts
towards me. I choose one.
How quickly the knowledge
dances
from one windless bough
to another

OCTOBER

Butter
flies in mid
October

Wasps full of sleep
crawl
over the red quilt
of leaves

You've been dead
two days.
Already a small spider
has built his net

from rim to handle
of your white
enamel
shaving mug

DAD

I thought you should know
I've planted

your alarm clocks,
your mug and razor

and your old Cruikshanks
cycling shoes

between the compost
and the clutter of dead

rhubarb. Somehow
it seemed the proper

thing to do,
rather than just

turning them out
to the bad jokes

of the bin men
without so much

as a thanks
for everything

GARLANDS

A wet Saturday in Cardiff,
mid-November.
Scabs of trodden chip paper

on the treacherous paving slabs.
The café crowded.
The wall a blur of boats

in Pwllheli harbour
facing a pallid still-life
with mandolin and miscellaneous fruits.

Above, a gilded chandelier
preens itself in the stacked coffee-pots.
A fog of blues

unfurls from a hidden speaker.
In the window opposite, the hats
are a mumbled confession of brown.

Over a cafetière of stiff Java,
I reflect that if it were
to come at all, it would choose

just such a drowned moment,
settling like unseasonable snow
in the brief blank between Cleo and Fats

SUNRISE

At the path's edge
a snail's dawn

cold spiral
on a grass blade

WINTER

Your body's reverting to wild,
your hair bramble,
your memory winter:
you can no longer tell
where you will be
when you talk to someone.

There's something about
a crazy woman in hospital
with a private line to the police
and the time you fell over
in the rockery and there was no one
to hear you shout,
then a bit about next door's
dog which went lame
and the spiralling
violence
and now hospital again
and how you got hopelessly lost
looking for the ladies' room
in the long flickering
corridors

                now there's
a gap you can't fill
you notice the backs
of your hands patched and runnelled
like limestone, your fingers
are off on a secret journey of their own
you watch a moment then
lose interest the wind's
rising and you haven't the heart
to call them home

GOING

It's the crunch:
we trundle the last threadbare scenery over the gravel:
battered wicker chair,
two cracked sycamore bookends
with owls, a dumb replica
of the liberty bell, a cigar
box of blackened pennies
with the Queen illegible.

Your man has dropped over the edge of the world
    forever.
What can I give you
to make up for this absolute
zero
poisoning your store of mornings?

The car nuzzles at the gate.
I cram everything in,
click you into the front seat,
slam the door.
Through the wound-up window you mouth:
Is it home where I'm going?
Am I married to anyone?

ROOTS

Auntie Edie's been moved into a home,
she kept phoning everybody up asking
if they'd got her husband and he's been
dead three years.
Of course nobody's interested
now they've got their hands on her money.
The deer keep jumping the back fence
and eating the heads off all my daffodils
and that fir tree is getting its roots
into the drains, there's no way
to stop it, one day we'll all wake up
and there'll be roots coming through
all the plugholes. She kept telling everyone
we'd stolen her pension money
well you can't put up with that
sort of thing can you? Of course Jack
won't say anything he'd rather just
sit back and watch everything go to ruin.
Imagine, roots as thick as my waist,
if we'd left them all we wouldn't
have an inch to call our own.
Well it's terrible when it's your own sister
and everybody's looking at each other.
Isn't it lovely sitting here just drinking in
the silence? My battery's going again,
what is it today? If it's Friday
it's fish

MEANING

is finally running out.
No matter how you plead,
this state of the art
opener will not mesh
with the Smedley's jumbo size
processed garden peas.

You grope tearfully for change
in a biscuit tin
brooding with blank moons;
carry the mush of cake
crumbs left from the funeral
as far as the bird table

then forget why.
I stand at the door encouraging
a terrified animal.
'Try raising the left first,
then the right,' I suggest.
'Try taking a deep breath.'

Now it's the turn of the new
minimalist quartz clock
on top of the TV.
'What do all those
numbers mean?' you ask.
'Are they time?'

WRITING EXERCISE

Sasanaratna is reading his ten-minute writing.
Everyone knows what's coming.

The birds in the eaves hush their chatter.
The clock on the wall stops,

The sun wonders whether to come out or
discreetly wait till it's over,

We all wonder how long it will take.
He builds up to it slowly, like a summer storm gathering.

The tension is unbearable.
The next line, surely.

Maybe he won't do it this time.
Then it comes: four frayed ribbons of pale lightning:

Help! Help! Help! Help!
The room's drenched in laughter.

We hold out our pads.
Our words become violet blotches of gratitude

BLOOD

A lake of bright blood
overflowing from the cistern.
I stare up at it a long time,
trying to decide who it means.

There are stars out there, burning
at inconceivable distances,
that know the moment
and place of my death.

There are cats
still as standing stones
that gaze at nothing year after year,
and disappear without ever giving a sign.

There are spiders
that crouch
for months in deep corners
and never miss a movement.

Suddenly I know it means me.
I have to eat it,
eat it whole in one gulp,
let it slide inside me like intelligent cream,

like alien skin rippling home,
so I can climb again whole
into the world,
holding my dread by the hand,

and tell him
the fat corner spiders
that know everything
really know nothing;

that the blood in the radio
is a lake of sweet knowledge;
that memory means holding hands
with the earth's naked

till our skin is an infinite window;
that the stars are boats anchored inside us,
prows quivering,
burning to be gone

'IN THE DARK WITH THE TRUTH'

There's a small unfurnished room to let
somewhere between my lungs
and my pelvis. It changes its address
constantly, moving at greatly varying speeds
so I can never locate it.

In the room is a word
that won't be written down, but
offers itself like a black sail at midnight,
rippling without a sound,
so I can never see the shape of it.

In the word is a memory
that shifts in and out of sunlight
like a noon gazelle,
or a rainbow in a squall
so I can never see the colour of it.

In the memory is a secret path
that twists forever through the world
kindling whatever it touches.
But there's no map of it,
and its surface won't support so much as a feather.

Yet without it my body's a furnace,
my mind interstellar space at absolute zero.

How to find it?

Switch off the day,
let the brain desert its masters,
pull out logic's plug.

Then choose a small, unspectacular kindness
(the sort so common it would never be missed)
and pursue it as far as it will take you,
in whatever direction it chooses,
without question.

Then open the squat, rain-soaked gate
of the morning, sit
and listen.
The word will be waiting: write it

SUNBURST

I'm perplexed
that I can't make her come
by wishing, or stay longer
than she wants.

Just now she glanced
the rim of this strait-laced
salt cellar
almost blinding me

with her nakedness.
Now she's a brightening
on the chair back, that looks
nothing at all

like the face of a girl
who, years ago
drove me out of my wits
in a smoke-black town

whose name's already a blur
in the mish-mash of dialects
I took for
the real thing

ALL THE CHILDREN

In this snake track, lean and wind-scribbled
in this night feathered earth

in the lee of furred rocks
in the shrivelled hands of tumbleweed
beached against the screen door

at the speechless end of a love affair
after the last kiss has turned to ice

where the road runs out to castles of spear-grass
in the hour when great rivers go dark

in the north light freighted with snow
in the weightless afternoon moment
when the driver turns off the engine

in the prairies of hours
in the train siren torn by wind
in the shy, listening boundaries

in the stopped face of the Indian woman
in the impossible velvet

in letting go of arriving
in not pursuing
in the absence of the rescuer

between the thought   and its twilight sister
I look for you

DRY FALLS

Sitting on
a rock
in the desert

afternoon sun
staining
the grass;

nothing
has stirred
for a thousand years

I pick up
a stone: it stares
back

TALKING WITH BROKEN OBJECTS

At a stroke, the red
kerbstones come alive with alien lettering.

Trains that have laboured through the night
settle and cool by shadowed platforms

The smooth ships are fuelled and loaded
but no one arrives to release them.

What is it that can't be thought?
What tugs us back year after year

to the same river bed
where the same stones glitter,

show us their perfect figures
and do not sing to us?

HOW THE DAY STARTS HERE

All you do is sit still
and let everything begin:

a man with a grey beard throws
out some garbage.
A blue bird glints.
A small girl hops between bars
of shadow.
Leaves rock themselves awake
in the creeping warmth.

Where to go from here?
How remember what needs remembering?
How fit this hour into
the long necklace of knowing?

Now the sun hides.
The day is balanced
between grey and blue.
The traffic waits.

Just for this moment I can choose

WAITING FOR THE FERRY
FROM BAINBRIDGE ISLAND

'The directionless learn only by moving.' (Roethke: Proverbs of Purgatory)

Nothing to do for the rest
of the afternoon. Breakfasts are
over. The waitress contemplates
the five o'clock commute home.
The ferry sprawls into the bay
like a yawning snail.

I'm a third of the globe from you.
Dusk here
is darkest before dawn in England.
Maybe you're sleepless,
teasing out a snagged dream.
Maybe a far dog's bark nuzzled you awake.

Between us I sense the delicacy
of deserts, their dim coral
stretching moonless and unvisited,
their stones aching to face a star.
The ferry booms again,
slinks through shafts of silky zinc,

trembles to grey. Something deeper
than distance
tugs us to this edge, to stare
barefoot at the future, guess
what it will demand for passage,
and hope it loves us

HUMMINGBIRD

Perhaps this is how prayer begins:
a flicker above the shallow feeder,
a shadow half-arrived,
an actinic glint –
a hundred per cent
faith, zero doubt.

The sky droops.
What should I wish for?
A fresh start, minus history,
more love, less thought?

But some lever in the world might tip
sideways, a quiet balance lost,
and a hundred years from now, perhaps
a civilization or two is dust.

Maybe if I got my way, his
would go out; and we need
his lack of need, his sleek, split-
second economy.

Now his brilliance loops
elsewhere, his deft needlepoint
threads another galaxy.
I slump with toast near the tall cactus
and dream

REFUGE

'It is a dreadful thing to feel that all one possesses is slipping away' (PASCAL)

In the midst of his beauty something
is exploding. The trees
have gone down too far
and stopped dead.
Under their crimson the leaves
are going out, like a child's stifled
cry under concrete.

Memory forgets its pledge.
If he slows down enough, the shock-
wave from the future
reaches him like a hissing bible.
Conversations are forked with warnings.
Flames erupt violet between syntax.
The sky's rivers bulge black.

Is it only the year,
the things un-nurtured, un-
grieved for? Or worse:
the drying of deep wells,
an outcry from a place unvisited?

There is left only music,
like a great protecting arm of quiet.
For a second sweetness floods
upward, softens the world,
before his fingers find its edge
and freeze

SAN FRANCISCO BLUES

or, the man with a raging fire in his belly considers enrolling in a course on cross-cultural hysteria

1 I always have the same dream. It starts in my right brain and then halfway through moves on to someone else's without any explanation.

2 Every morning around 4 a.m. an anguished cry escapes from my throat, but no one can tell me what it means.

3 I often feel hunger but can't tell who it belongs to.

4 The kind of moon I'm looking for is lemon-shaped, deep mauve in colour, and inlaid with bright pink stripes, and makes you feel good whenever you look at it.

5 I tried therapy last summer but it gave me a headache.

6 I have developed some state-of-the-art software that can tell me precisely where the flames will be in one second, one minute, or one year from now. Why does this knowledge give me no peace?

7 One night I heard a voice which told me to unscrew all the fluorescent tubes from the subway and carry them outside so that once in their lives they could see a sunrise.

8 My work only makes sense when viewed in a certain light, at a certain hour, from a certain angle, and with a completely open mind. And then not always.

9 'I started it, and I worked about an hour on it, and a dealer came in from Palo Alto and looked at it, and he said he liked it just the way it was and not to work on it, so I didn't.' *(From the amateur artists' annual show catalog 96/97)*

NORWICH, FEBRUARY

Sunlit Marlboro
pack, stamped
with someone's patterned heel;
ripped cover

of a men's weekly
glancing out of wetness;
a spent ball pen's
obsolete shaft

not yet crushed
by a bus wheel;
moss on the milky flint
of the medieval

walls levelled within
slicks of concrete;
and way below
where the slow river bends

the cathedral spire
weathered but
clean as a new engine
waiting for God to spring

into the driving seat,
flick the ignition
in the old assured way,
ease down the pedal

WHY THE RAIN MAKES PUDDLES

not because
the road is made badly

but so we can notice
the moon

sailing free
when we are downcast

MOUSE POTATO

There is a mouse in the affairs of men.
Nobody loves an old mouse.
A mouse in time saves nine.
It's an ill wind that never turns over a new mouse.
Go to work on a mouse.
Take your mouse and git out of town mister.
Whose mouse is it anyway?
A mouse too far.
A mouse for all seasons.
A one mouse town.
A mouse in the family.
The mouse at the end of the universe.
The mouse of the Baskervilles.
The Ballad of the Sad mouse.
The return of the Mouse.
Lady Chatterley's mouse.
Beethoven's mouse.
Flaubert's mouse.
Tender is the mouse.
A mouse before sunrise.
What kind of mouse am I?
The mouse who was Tuesday.
To take up arms against a sea of mice.
A mouse by any other name.
A fool and his mouse are easily parted.
Cometh the hour, cometh the mouse.
And Jesus said, whosoever is without sin, let him cast the first
    mouse.
Where there's a will there's a mouse.
Those who live by the mouse shall perish by the mouse.

Who's a pretty mouse then?
Gimme a real mouse.
My kingdom for a mouse.
Twentieth Century Mouse.
Essex Mouse.
Mouse Friday.
The Russia Mouse.
The Third Mouse.
A little mouse music.
Midnight Mouse.
Put out more mice.
Hippopotamouse.
What Mouse?
Mouse and Garden.
Wag the mouse.

DUSK

There's something I need, that never shows
itself.
I imagine it – a distant lamp,
the fictions of ice
on tall panes –
but already the heel is swinging down
insanely jealous.

The curtains are still half-open:
sodium's goose-flesh bleeds in the glass.

What if winter were a gateway
to its lair
high among pine-needles and rain-
etched limestone?
And what if memory's surrender
were the price?

I am free
to go there. Nothing prevents me but
what I have become.

But already the heel arcs down,
the leaf's intensities already beyond reach;

and for an instant, my father's voice
edging across, etched
with need,
struggling with its curse,
its seven generations of shame

INDEX

244

248

The Windhorse symbolizes the energy of the enlightened mind carrying the Three Jewels – the Buddha, the Dharma, and the Sangha – to all sentient beings.

Buddhism is one of the fastest-growing spiritual traditions in the Western world. Throughout its 2,500-year history, it has always succeeded in adapting its mode of expression to suit whatever culture it has encountered.

Windhorse Publications aims to continue this tradition as Buddhism comes to the West. Today's Westerners are heirs to the entire Buddhist tradition, free to draw instruction and inspiration from all the many schools and branches. Windhorse publishes works by authors who not only understand the Buddhist tradition but are also familiar with Western culture and the Western mind.

For orders and catalogues contact

WINDHORSE PUBLICATIONS	WINDHORSE BOOKS	WEATHERHILL INC
11 PARK ROAD	P O BOX 574	41 MONROE TURNPIKE
BIRMINGHAM	NEWTON	TRUMBULL
B13 8AB	NSW 2042	CT 06611
UK	AUSTRALIA	USA

Windhorse Publications is an arm of the Friends of the Western Buddhist Order, which has more than sixty centres on five continents. Through these centres, members of the Western Buddhist Order offer regular programmes of events for the general public and for more experienced students. These include meditation classes, public talks, study on Buddhist themes and texts, and 'bodywork' classes such as t'ai chi, yoga, and massage. The FWBO also runs several retreat centres and the Karuna Trust, a fund-raising charity that supports social welfare projects in the slums and villages of India.

Many FWBO centres have residential spiritual communities and ethical businesses associated with them. Arts activities are encouraged too, as is the development of strong bonds of friendship between people who share the same ideals. In this way the FWBO is developing a unique approach to Buddhism, not simply as a set of techniques, less still as an exotic cultural interest, but as a creatively directed way of life for people living in the modern world.

If you would like more information about the FWBO please write to

LONDON BUDDHIST CENTRE
51 ROMAN ROAD
LONDON
E2 0HU
UK

ARYALOKA
HEARTWOOD CIRCLE
NEWMARKET
NH 03857
USA

FWBO (ARTS) is an organization that promotes the appreciation and practice of the arts in a spiritual context. It is a registered charity and organizes arts retreats, workshops, classes, seminars, and performances. FWBO (ARTS) was inspired by the thought and writings of Sangharakshita, the founder and teacher of the Friends of the Western Buddhist Order. A writer and poet, he has examined the links between the spiritual and the artistic life; in particular, in his book of essays *The Religion of Art*, he argues that true art is a communication of spiritual values.

Rising Fire is the publishing wing of FWBO (ARTS). The Rising Fire logo takes its symbolism from the stupa, a Buddhist architectural form representing the elements and different kinds of energy, as well as spiritual development. The triangular shape represents the element of fire. It could be said that fire, being the element of liberated energy, symbolizes inspiration and thus is the sphere of the artist.

ALSO FROM WINDHORSE

SANGHARAKSHITA

COMPLETE POEMS 1941–1994

Sangharakshita has dedicated himself to helping people transform
their lives not only through his work as a Buddhist teacher but also
through the medium of verse, for in his poetry he combines the
sensitivity of the poet with the vision born of a life of contemplation
and uncompromising spiritual practice.

Here we have the opportunity to listen to a unique voice and to be
uplifted by the reflections of an extraordinary person and an accom-
plished teacher.

528 pages, hardback
ISBN 0 904766 70 5
£17.99/$34.95

SANGHARAKSHITA

THE RELIGION OF ART

Just as beauty is truth, and truth beauty, the spiritual life and the artistic life are inextricably linked.

A work of art not only expresses its creator's clearest insight and most refined emotion, it also acts as a means through which we may experience something of the beauty he has perceived. Properly approached, both religion and art lead to an expansion of consciousness, a state of heightened awareness and understanding in which, ultimately, the limiting boundaries of 'self' no longer hold.

In this collection of essays, Sangharakshita offers a manifesto for a radical appraisal of art and religion.

172 pages
ISBN 0 904766 31 4
£6.99/$13.95

SANGHARAKSHITA

HERCULES AND THE BIRDS

'My poems constitute a sort of spiritual autobiography, sketchy indeed, but perhaps revealing, or at least suggesting, aspects of my life which would not otherwise be known.'

Whether lamenting the mindless barbarity of Italy's Sunday afternoon huntsmen, contemplating the six 'realms' of existence, or reflecting on the muted spaciousness of the Norfolk countryside, Sangharakshita gives himself to verse with sensitivity, compassion, and a meticulous joy.

These poems are an excellent introduction to his verse writings. More than that: they are a unique introduction to the man himself.

64 pages
ISBN 0 904766 43 8
£3.95/$7.95

SANGHARAKSHITA

IN THE REALM OF THE LOTUS: A CONVERSATION
ABOUT ART, BEAUTY, AND THE SPIRITUAL LIFE

Is there a place for beauty and art in the spiritual life?

Sangharakshita has a reputation as a Buddhist scholar, prolific writer, and spiritual teacher – but he is also a visionary poet, dreamer, and lover of art.

In this remarkable interview – conducted by Olle Mallander for Finnish television – Sangharakshita leads us through his inner landscapes, early influences, and visionary experiences. His belief is that a true work of art offers us a symbol of spiritual communication - or even of divine inspiration. This interview provides a glimpse of the splendour of such communication.

72 pages, illustrated
ISBN 0 904766 72 1
£ 4.99/$8.95

SIR EDWIN ARNOLD

THE LIGHT OF ASIA

This inspiring poem by Sir Edwin Arnold (1832–1904), though written more than a hundred years ago, retains the power to move us in a way that no prose rendering of the life of the Buddha can. We cannot but admire the courage, determination, and self-sacrifice of the Indian prince who, out of compassion, left his palace to find a remedy for the sufferings of the world.

192 pages, with glossary
ISBN 1 899579 19 2
£ 9.99/$19.95

PARAMANANDA

CHANGE YOUR MIND:

A PRACTICAL GUIDE TO BUDDHIST MEDITATION

Buddhism is based on the truth that, with effort, we can change the way we are. But how? Among the many methods Buddhism has to offer, meditation is the most direct. It is the art of getting to know one's own mind and learning to encourage what is best in us.

This is an accessible and thorough guide to meditation, based on traditional material but written in a light and modern style. Colourfully illustrated with anecdotes and tips from the author's experience as a meditator and teacher, it also offers refreshing inspiration to seasoned meditators.

208 pages, with photographs
ISBN 0 904766 81 0
£8.99/$17.95

258

TEJANANDA

THE BUDDHIST PATH TO AWAKENING

The word Buddha means 'one who is awake'. In this accessible
introduction, Tejananda alerts us to the Buddha's wake-up call, illus-
trating how the Buddhist path can help us develop a clearer mind and
a more compassionate heart.

Drawing on over twenty years experience of Buddhist meditation
and study, Tejananda gives us a straightforward and encouraging
description of the path of the Buddha and his followers – the path that
leads ultimately to our own 'awakening'.

224 pages with diagrams
ISBN 1 899579 02 8
£8.99/$17.95